D0148593

LORNA WING MD MRCPsych

Autistic Children

A GUIDE FOR PARENTS AND PROFESSIONALS

Second Edition

BRUNNER/MAZEL, Publishers • New York

Library of Congress Cataloging in Publication Data

Wing, Lorna.
Autistic children.

Bibliography: p.
Includes index.
1. Autism. 2. Autistic children—Care and treatment.
I. Title.
RJ506.A9W52 1985 649'.154 84-29276
ISBN 0-87630-391-2

Published by
BRUNNER/MAZEL, INC.
19 Union Square West
New York, N.Y. 10003

Originally published in the United Kingdom
by Constable Publishers, London

MANUFACTURED IN THE UNITED STATES OF AMERICA

Preface to Second Edition

Since the first edition of this book was written, there have been some advances in knowledge concerning the impairments of psychological function underlying the autistic behaviour pattern. More evidence has accumulated that certain organic conditions tend to be associated with autism, though the precise way in which those causes operate to produce the typical behaviour pattern remains unknown. It has also become clear that the methods of teaching and managing behaviour problems appropriate for autistic children are also helpful for the wider group who have autistic features, but not the full classic syndrome.

Follow-up studies have confirmed that most autistic children remain handicapped all their lives, the majority of them severely so. For this reason, there is more emphasis in this book on the need for residential care and sheltered occupation for autistic adults, and the special problems of the most severely handicapped groups.

It will be evident that this edition is less hopeful in tone than the first, but it is only when the facts are fully understood and accepted that constructive planning for the future is possible.

L.W.
1980

Foreword

At a time when one easily gets discouraged about therapy of the syndrome first described by Leo Kanner, "Early Infantile Autism," it is good news to hear the voice of Lorna Wing, M.D., DPM, in "Autistic Children." This book is unique in that, based on solid scientific data, it addresses parents in a competent, lucid, detailed manner about the condition of their children and how to help them. Its subtitle, "Guide for Parents," is modest indeed if one considers the wealth of professional information that it brings to the attention of the reader.

Over a decade of research on the subject has gone into the preparation of this book, in addition to the vast experience of its writer. The symptomatology is comprehensively covered with the object of bringing out the essentials, their significance and their role in the therapeutic process. Therapy, in the case of autism, must come from *outside*—education rather than interpretation of inner life. This is a strong point made by Dr. Wing: psychotherapy and psychoanalysis have proved ineffectual because of the language and symbolism deficiencies characteristic of the children. With immeasurable patience and minute detail, she outlines techniques to be used, step by step, covering every form of behavior and disability encountered in these children. "Techniques" is too formal a word; one is tempted to say "practical suggestions."

The material, covering the individual pathology, its social connotations, its incidence in the (English) society, is aptly organized. The author's thoroughness in dealing with behavior anomalies is impressive, the more so as the uniform, typical picture on the one hand and the apparent diversity existing side by side make, nevertheless, for a definite, unmistakable pattern. This is often difficult of interpretation, even for the reasonably experienced therapist, owing to the subtle variations.

Differentiating from syndromes which are sometimes confused with autism is carefully analyzed. A chapter, "Comparisons with Other Childhood Handicaps and Problems," is devoted to this differential diagnosis ("congenital deafness—congenital aphasia—visual problems—mental retardation—elective mutism and some types of childhood psychoses"). Since many of the autistic children have made the round of specialists (pediatrics, neurology, ENT. etc.) prior to finally reaching a psychiatrist who may be familiar with the syndrome, this chapter is of considerable importance.

Lorna Wing's view of the problem is encouraging without being wildly optimistic. She stresses the necessary empathy of the educator, in addition to his or her acquaintance with the scientific data, for the education—not training—of these children.

The National Society for Autistic Children seems to be very active in England. Lorna Wing has been associated with its development and with the research concerning early childhood autism. The survey initiated in Middlesex County regarding the incidence in the general child population brought out some interesting facts: that about 6,000 children is the total number of autistic children in England, that in the 8-9-10 year old group tested (tested in toto, a fundamentally scientific approach) between four and five children in 10,000 are found to show autistic behavior, that three boys to one girl are affected. All of which is valuable knowledge.

Her observations and analysis of the autistic behavior and language have led her to formulate as a goal a slowly progressive development toward integration in society, via individual growth. The greatest accomplishment here may be the work done with the families, also with professional categories such as teachers, psychologists, speech therapists, pediatricians, psychiatrists, any and all individuals and institutions entrusted with the welfare of these children.

She treats the subject of etiology of the disease in a manner which is at once learned and clearly expressed for layman consumption, in a field where little is known to date. The subdivision of her chapter "Theories of Causes" includes two headings.

a. *Theories which suggest emotional causes*
b. *Theories which suggest physical causes*

Examining all hypotheses under these two headings, the weight of her conviction is on the side of the latter, physical or organic causes.

The last chapter "Services for Autistic Children" relates to services as they are available in England and what desirable improvements could be accomplished there, but even as such, they offer a guideline in what can be done in any country.

The value of this book for the parents of autistic children cannot be overestimated. I also have no reluctance to admit that I, with some clinical experience of early infantile autism, have learned and benefitted from the reading of this book.

J. LOUISE DESPERT, M.D.

Contents

Part I
Description of the children

1

Introduction

The mental and physical development of children can go wrong in many different ways, and sometimes this leads to difficult behaviour. Autism is one of the ways in which disturbed development may be shown. Autistic children appear at first sight to be strikingly different from normal children, and from children with the commoner kinds of childhood disabilities. However, each of the problems they show can be found in other handicapped children, especially in those who have one or more of the impairments affecting perception and language development. It is easier for parents to deal with the situation if they can see their child as handicapped, sharing problems with other handicapped children, but also remembering that he is first and foremost a child, with the same need as every other child for a home and family, love, security, guidance and a chance to develop his skills and positive assets to the full. Each autistic child has his own personality which determines the way he reacts to his handicaps and which makes him a unique individual. For these reasons, parents and others who work with these children do not like to hear them referred to as 'autistics', which suggests that the handicap is the only thing that matters. They are children who happen to be suffering from the condition known as early childhood autism.

DEFINITIONS

One of the biggest problems in writing about autistic children is that doctors and other professional people tend to differ in the words they use to describe and name the condition. The cause, or causes, of autism in children are, as yet, unknown, and there are no neat tests which can be used to make the diagnosis. Blood tests, X-rays, electro-encephalograms (that is, records of the electrical waves from the brain), and other physical examinations which are helpful in general medicine, cannot give a positive answer to the question 'Is this child autistic?', although they are sometimes necessary to detect or exclude other conditions which might be present. The only way to make a positive diagnosis is for the doctor to ask about the child's behaviour, in minute detail, from birth up to the time of examination, because the decision depends upon the presence or absence of a special pattern of behaviour.

In this situation, people look for theories to explain the children's odd behaviour, and the different names that are used are linked with some of the ideas that have been put forward. Professor Kanner suggested the name 'early infantile autism' because he believed that the aloofness and social withdrawal shown in the early years were the most important features. ('Autism', used in psychiatry to mean withdrawn and self-absorbed, comes from the Greek word 'autos', meaning 'self'.) Other workers refer to the condition as 'childhood schizophrenia', because they believe that it is a special form of the adult illness.* Others again have

* This theory is being discarded nowadays, for several reasons. Firstly, the symptoms of autism are different from those of schizophrenia. For example, delusions and hallucinations are important in the latter and never seen in the former, and the speech problems of autism are not at all the same as those found in some schizophrenic patients. Secondly, when autistic children grow up, they do not become schizophrenic adults. Thirdly, schizophrenic patients are more likely than average to have relatives who are also schizophrenic. Autistic children, on the other hand, have only the same chance of having a schizophrenic relative as the average (and some say the chance is less than average). The only similarity is that both schizophrenic adults and autistic children are very vulnerable to the effects of bad institutions, but this goes for other kinds of handicaps too.

used very general terms, such as 'childhood psychosis', 'severe emotional disturbance', 'non-communicating children' or 'exceptional children', but these labels can cover so many different behaviour patterns that they cause more problems than they solve.

In this book I shall try to avoid confusion over names by defining terms in simple concrete ways, and in some detail. There are many different ideas as to what a 'psychosis' is, but I shall use the label 'childhood psychosis' to cover all those conditions in which a child behaves most or all of the time in ways which are extremely strange and unpredictable, even considering his age and his level of intelligence. Many children who are backward act in a way which is strange for their physical age, but which is understandable if you know that they are mentally retarded. They are therefore not called psychotic. On the other hand, some children have patterns of behaviour which are unusual whatever their level of mental development and when this odd behaviour is continuous the children can be said to be psychotic. The term is a description and not an explanation of behaviour. Sometimes the cause of a childhood psychosis is known. It may be, for example, a brain tumour, some brain injury, or an infection in early childhood. More often, however, it is not possible to find any definite reason for the behaviour because, as yet, methods of examining the function of the brain are limited.

The term 'childhood psychosis' covers many different patterns of behaviour of which early childhood autism is one, and perhaps the commonest, example. The behaviour shown by autistic children will be described in detail in Chapter 4 below.

2

History

It seems likely that there have always been autistic children, although it is only since Kanner's paper in 1943 that they have been named as a group and thought of separately from other severely mentally handicapped children. Perhaps they were the reason for the legends of 'fairy changeling' children, in which the fairies were believed to steal away a human baby and leave a fairy child in its place. In some versions of the story the changeling was remarkably beautiful, but strange and remote from human kind.

In 1799 a French doctor, J. M. G. Itard, was given charge of a boy about twelve years old, known as Victor the 'Wild boy of Aveyron', who had been found wandering and living wild in the woods. The child's behaviour was very abnormal. Itard thought that he was handicapped because he had been isolated from humans from an early age. Pinel, another eminent doctor of the time, disagreed with Itard over this, and believed that the boy was severely mentally retarded from birth. Reading the story now, it is possible to see that Victor behaved like an autistic child. Some people have suggested that he was autistic because he was abandoned in infancy. It seems much more likely that he was separated from, or abandoned by, his parents in the troubled times following the French Revolution *because* he was autistic and difficult to manage, and not the other way round. Itard's story is most interesting and moving, and worth reading because of the way in which he set about teaching the boy.

Over a century later, in 1919, an American psychologist, Lightner Witmer, wrote an article about Don, a boy of two years and seven months, who also behaved like an autistic child, and who was accepted at Witmer's special school. Individual teaching over a long period helped this child to compensate for his handicaps.

Professor Kanner, in 1943, was the first person to describe these children as a special group. Since then interest has grown steadily. Many different theories of causes have been put forward, and the actual behaviour of the children has been observed in more detail. As a result of such studies, many workers now feel that Kanner's early childhood autism is not a specific and separate condition. Although the classically autistic child is easy to recognise, there are many more children with autistic features who do not show the full syndrome. The wider group of children has the same needs for a special type of education and management as the typically autistic child. This finding has implications for the estimation of numbers and the provision of services, as will be discussed in the next chapter.

In 1962, the first society for parents and interested professional workers was set up in the United Kingdom. Subsequently, such associations have been formed in many different countries. They have worked for wider recognition of the problem, earlier diagnosis, better services, and for more and better opportunities for special education. After some years of effort on behalf of the children, it became clear that most would need to live and work in a sheltered setting all their lives, so the voluntary societies are now concerned to develop day and residential centres for adults with autism and related conditions. Some progress has been made in all these fields, but there is still a long way to go.

3

How many children are autistic?

TYPICAL AUTISM

The first special study designed to answer this question was carried out in 1964 in the English county of Middlesex. Every child aged eight, nine or ten years whose home address was in the county was considered, whether or not he was known to have any mental or physical handicap. The results showed that between four and five children in every 10,000 in the age range studied had autistic behaviour. About half had the full classic behaviour pattern described by Kanner. This means that their behavioural abnormalities included the two features Kanner considered to be fundamental. These are social aloofness and indifference to others, especially other children, in the early years of childhood (though this may become much less marked with increasing age), and elaborate repetitive routines instead of the imaginative, flexible, pretend play of normal children. The other half had the syndrome in less marked form but still with enough of the typical picture to be diagnosed as autistic.

Two more studies, one in Aarhus county, Denmark, and one in the Camberwell area of London, England, used similar definitions of early childhood autism to those in the Middlesex research, and gave the same result. The important point about all three surveys is that the workers made their own diagnoses and did not count only those children seen and diagnosed as autistic by psychiatric clinics.

CHILDREN WITH AUTISTIC FEATURES

The Camberwell study also included a wider range of children. Every child in the area aged under 15 years who had any difficulty in taking part in two-way social interactions or who had repetitive, stereotyped activities, whether these were simple or elaborate, or who had impairment of comprehension and use of non-verbal and verbal communication was examined. This definition included the autistic children but also covered many who had 'autistic features'. For example, there were very severely handicapped children who were markedly aloof and rejected all approaches from other children and who had no pretend play at all, but whose repetitive behaviour consisted of such simple activities as rocking, teeth grinding, or gazing at bright lights. Another group included those who had never been socially aloof, but whose social interactions were odd, naive and one-sided and whose social behaviour was not affected by the responses or interests of the people they approached. These children also had repetitive activities, sometimes consisting of a fascination with a particular topic such as astronomy, railway time-tables, plumbing, or monsters from outer space. A few children were found who lacked genuine two-way social interaction, but who did develop a kind of pretend play. However, this was limited to one or two themes, and was repeated endlessly without variation.

The problem of social interaction arises from a lack, or a very limited grasp of the highly complex and subtle rules governing human communication. It is different from that seen in emotionally disturbed or delinquent children, who understand these rules but respond to other people in neurotic or anti-social ways.

From the available evidence, it appears that the number of children with typical or nearly typical autism is fairly predictable, at least in industrialised societies, but that the number with autistic features varies from one area to another, for reasons that need to be investigated. The range for the latter is approximately seven to fifteen in every 10,000 children. Adding those with typical autism and those with autistic features gives a total of twelve to twenty per 10,000 children aged below fifteen years.

AGE OF ONSET

Kanner at first believed that classic autism was always present from birth, and he therefore named it early *infantile* autism. Later he observed the same syndrome in children who appeared to have had a year or two of normal development before becoming autistic, and later writers have extended this to three or even four years. For this reason, the term early *childhood* autism seems more appropriate and will be used in this book.

The wider range of children with autistic features studied in the Camberwell survey were all abnormal from birth or within the first five years of life, the great majority having an onset before three years of age. The whole range of these behaviour patterns, including typical autism, is sometimes referred to, collectively, as the 'early childhood psychoses'.

PSYCHOSES IN LATER CHILDHOOD

Children can develop psychoses after the age of five, but these are different from those seen in early childhood. In most cases they are the psychiatric conditions seen far more often in adult life, such as schizophrenia, mania or psychotic depression. Such problems are extremely rare in childhood. The early childhood psychoses are, by comparison, more common.

SEX RATIO IN AUTISM

Boys are affected more often than girls. Kanner found four times as many boys among children with the classic autistic syndrome, but in the Middlesex study the ratio was a little less than three boys to one girl. There are also more boys among children with autistic features; though, overall, this difference is not as marked as in classic autism.

ASSOCIATED MEDICAL CONDITIONS

More than a third of all children with autism or autistic behaviour have a history of some medical condition that affects the brain, either inherited, or occurring before, during, or after birth (see Chapter 5). Approximately one-third have had at least one epileptic fit by the time they reach adult life. The more severely handicapped the child, the more likely it is that some medical condition will be found to account for the handicaps.

Kanner thought that children who seemed to have abnormalities of the brain produced by a physical cause should not be put into the same group as those with classic early childhood autism. The problem in accepting this idea is that better methods of examining the central nervous system have been developed since Kanner first defined the autistic syndrome. Some children with very characteristic autistic behaviour can now be shown to have organic brain damage. If the children are followed up into adult life, signs of such damage may become clear, although unsuspected in early childhood. A few post-mortem examinations have also shown abnormalities of the brain undiagnosed in life.

Sometimes children with autism or autistic features have additional handicaps such as deafness, blindness or, rarely, cerebral palsy (spasticity). It is even possible to find autistic behaviour in a child with Down's syndrome (once known as mongolism), although most such children are very sociable, communicative and have pretend play.

USEFUL SKILLS

All children with autism and related conditions are mentally handicapped because they lack the essential quality needed for normal intelligence and adaptability to the demands of life – that is, sufficient imagination to think about the past and present and to make some appropriate plans for the future. However, they do vary greatly in the number of useful skills they possess.

These skills can be measured by using certain psychological tests which explore non-verbal, practical abilities and rote memory. From the results it is possible to classify the children on a rough scale of severity. Nearly four-fifths of the total group of children with early childhood psychosis function in the severely retarded range, and only a tiny proportion have skills in the normal range of ability.

The children with typical or nearly typical autism tend to have higher levels of skill than those with autistic features, of whom some are profoundly retarded with virtually no skills at all. Even among the typically autistic group about half function as severely retarded, although they have some useful visuo-spatial skills.

PARENTS' OCCUPATIONS

Almost all the autistic children seen by Kanner had fathers who were of higher intelligence and educational and occupational level than the average. He believed that this was a special feature of typical autism. Some workers argued that this was a false impression. They thought it was due to the fact that better educated people might prefer the d agnosis of autism to that of mental retardation and would have the knowledge and determination to find their way to Kanner's clinic.

Many, but not all, studies of autistic children seen at various different centres have found the same tendency in the parents' occupations, though never to the same marked extent as that described by Kanner. But any sample based on a clinic may be biased by special selection factors. The three studies mentioned before, in which all children in one area were screened, and the diagnosis of autism was made by the research workers, gave the opportunity of looking at the occupation of the parents of a (presumably) unbiased group of autistic children. The Middlesex survey found evidence of higher intelligence, education and occupation among the parents of the most typically autistic children, whereas the surveys in Aarhus and Camberwell did not.

The question with regard to typical autism remains open. For children with autistic features, no particular theories about the parents' occupations have been put forward, and the Camberwell survey found no special trends among this group.

SPECIAL NEEDS

When the first National Society for Autistic Children was started, many members assumed that the special methods of education and management they advocated were right only for classically autistic children. As time went on, it became clear that children with autistic features, even if they did not have typical autism, also benefited from the same kind of educational approach and their parents needed similar advice on management.

This brings up the question of whether it is worthwhile considering autism as separate from other kinds of mental handicaps. My own answer to this is that it is important to identify children who have severe impairment of social communication and development of imagination, as described here. These include the autistic group and those with autistic features.

They differ from normal and non-autistic retarded children because they learn little or nothing from social interaction in groups with other children or from pretend play, and they find it difficult or impossible to generalise from one situation to another. They need an organised, structured routine, a largely non-verbal approach to teaching skills, and much individual attention. These requirements may be met in various different settings, including those for mixed handicaps as well as specialised schools and units, but, wherever the child is placed, it is necessary to recognise the nature of his problems and how he differs from other children. This is true at all levels of skill, from profound retardation up to normal non-verbal ability.

For convenience, in the rest of this book, I shall use the term autistic children to cover children with typical autism and those with autistic features.

4

The behaviour of autistic children

In this chapter I shall describe the behaviour seen in typical autism. Each autistic child is an individual and is different from every other child with autism or autistic features, so the description should be taken as a general guide and not as an exact specification for diagnosis. Children vary in how much of the full behaviour pattern they show, how severely they are affected, and whether or not they have any other medical conditions. Also, changes occur with increasing age. Every child has his own personality which somehow shines through despite his handicaps. Nevertheless, the common problems affecting social communication and imagination can be recognised behind all the variations.

BABYHOOD

Some babies who will become autistic children appear to develop normally for a time, and their parents do not notice anything unusual in the first year or two (although careful questioning may show that these children, as babies, showed little active interest in their surroundings). Other babies give their parents cause for concern almost from birth. Sometimes mothers say that they felt something was wrong within the first few days, but they usually cannot tell why they had this feeling. Feeding problems are fairly common, and some of the babies do not suck well.

There seem to be two kinds of autistic babies, among those who are obviously abnormal from birth. Some scream a great deal during both day and night, especially on waking from sleep, and cannot be comforted or soothed. The only way to stop the crying may be a ride in a pram or a car and the screaming usually starts again when the motion ceases. The baby may be stiff and hard to cuddle, and may fight against everything, including being washed, dressed and changed.

The second kind of autistic baby is placid and undemanding, content to lie quietly in his pram all day. Sometimes mothers feel that a child of this kind does not know when he is hungry because he never cries for food and would starve unless fed as a routine. This type of child is less exhausting than the first, and less obviously worrying, but parents become concerned as time goes on and the child does not become more active.

One of the things most often noticed by mothers is that their autistic baby never lifts up his arms or makes himself ready to be picked up. When lifted up the children do not snuggle down comfortably in their mother's arms, and later on do not grip with their hands and knees if carried pick-a-back.

Some autistic babies lie in their prams and scratch or tap on the cover for long periods of time, and some rock or bang their heads when left alone. They may be fascinated by lights, or by anything that shines and twinkles. On the other hand they seem uninterested in the things which catch the attention of a normal baby as he grows and develops. Autistic babies do not lean out of their prams in eager curiosity to look at people and animals and the passing traffic, nor do they try to attract their mother's attention to these things by pointing and making excited noises.

This lack of interest makes parents wonder if their child is severely mentally retarded, but they usually do not accept this possibility because autistic babies tend to smile, cut their teeth, sit up, crawl and walk at the usual ages, and gain weight normally, once early feeding problems have passed. Sometimes the milestones are later than normal, but this is more likely in a child who has other handicaps as well as autism. However, mothers may say that their baby smiled when tickled, cuddled or bounced up and down, but not when looking at someone's face. They may also remember that he did not bother to sit up even when he was able to, apparently because the world was of little interest to him. A number of the children stand up and walk round the furniture at the right time, but may be reluctant to let go and walk without support until many months after the usual age.

TWO TO FIVE YEARS OF AGE

This is the stage when autistic behaviour is most obvious. If a child has been autistic from birth, it may be a long time before his parents put their fears and suspicions into words, but they usually become seriously worried by the time he is two or three years old, when he is most difficult to manage. If, on the other hand, the child has appeared normal from birth but has a marked change of behaviour occurring over a few weeks, his parents are likely to be alerted much more quickly to the gravity of the problem.

Young autistic children, especially those who have no other handicaps which might affect their appearance, seem to be physically healthy and are often unusually attractive. They have large eyes which do not look directly at other people. They seem to be aloof and unaffected by the world, interested only in some special object such as a smooth pebble or an empty box. If this object is lost, or if a familiar routine is disturbed, then the quiet remote child becomes a bundle of fury until his temper tantrum expires as quickly as it started – as if a tap had been turned off.

These 'typical' symptoms are so striking in early childhood that they tend to attract all the attention. This is a pity because this odd behaviour follows from other, more fundamental, handicaps, and it is impossible to understand and help an autistic child unless you know about the underlying problems which make it so hard for him to understand the world. The best way to describe them is to take each area of difficulty in turn and give some examples actually observed in autistic children. For the sake of simplicity I shall concentrate upon the kind of child who was autistic from birth or early babyhood.

PROBLEMS IN UNDERSTANDING THE WORLD

i *Unusual responses to sounds*

People often think that an autistic child is deaf because he tends to ignore very loud sounds, and not even blink if someone drops a pile of plates behind him. His parents usually know that he can hear because they notice that he turns round at once if, for example, a sweet is unwrapped behind him (that is, if he likes the kinds of sweets that are wrapped in paper). In 1799 Itard wrote about Victor: 'Of all his senses the ear appeared least sensitive. It was found, nevertheless that the sound of a cracking walnut or other favourite eatable never failed to make him turn round . . . yet this same organ showed itself insensible to the loudest of noises and the explosion of firearms.'

A child may be fascinated by some sounds such as that made by friction-drive toys or the ringing of a bell. Yet again he may find some sounds intensely distressing and will cover his ears and cringe away from the roar of a motor bike or the barking of a dog (though the children never seem to be sensitive to their own screams and shouts). These different responses may be seen in the same child within a short space of time.

ii *Difficulties in understanding speech*

A young autistic child's response to speech is just as unusual as the way he reacts to other sounds. Around one year of age, when a normal child loves to hear his mother speak to him and shows his delight with his whole body, the autistic child pays no more attention to speech than to any other noise. On the whole he ignores it, although a loud shout may make him distressed, or he may be fascinated by a gentle whisper. He seems unaware that speech has a meaning, although he may attend if he hears one of the few words he knows that are linked with things he likes ('sweet', 'dinner', 'orange drink'). It may be some years before he learns to come when his own name is called. At this stage he does not obey any verbal instructions, listen to any warnings, or comprehend if he is scolded. It is easy to see that bringing up an autistic child presents many problems.

Later on, usually near the age of five, many autistic children begin to acquire some limited comprehension of speech. They will obey simple instructions such as 'Put on your coat' or 'Come to dinner'. Later still they may be able to understand enough to 'Give this to Daddy', as long as Father is in the same room. Any complication (such as too many instructions in the same sentence) will confuse the child, so that he becomes angry or upset or else withdraws and does nothing. An older child who likes to help may do the wrong thing in response to a complex sentence. One little girl was asked to 'Bring Mummy your jumper which is on the chair in your bedroom'. The child trotted upstairs and after several minutes staggered in with the chair.

iii *Difficulties when talking*

Some autistic children never speak, but remain mute all their lives. Others (probably slightly more than half) do learn to say at least a few words, although they almost always begin much later than normal. They usually start by repeating words spoken by other people, especially the last word or the last few words of a sentence. Often the exact accent of the speaker may be copied, and the pitch of his voice.

The repetition of words seems to have little meaning for the child, and this empty echoing (like a parrot) is called 'echolalia'. Some children repeat words or phrases they have heard in the past and this is called 'delayed echolalia'. It occasionally happens that a child will produce one of these echoed phrases at an appropriate moment. For example, he might have a habit of saying 'You've left the door open' over and over again. Occasionally this will fit the situation and it will appear that the child knows what he is saying. It is easy to be misled into thinking that the child understands more than he really does, unless you know him well and realise that he repeats the things other people have said whether or not they are appropriate.

Some children never pass this stage, but others move on to the next, when they begin to say some words and phrases they work out for themselves, and which do have meaning. At first a child will name things that he wants, such as 'sweetie', 'drink', 'ice-cream'. He may then, after months or years, go on to use phrases. It is easy to tell the difference between a phrase that the child is echoing because he has heard it used by someone else and a phrase he has made up himself. The first comes out quickly and easily in the tones of the original speaker and often with good grammar. The second is produced with painful effort, and with many mistakes in grammar and word meanings. As with normal people learning a foreign language, autistic children find difficulty with the little linking words such as 'in', 'on', 'under', 'before' and 'because'. They may leave them out altogether, saying for example 'want dinner' 'go car shops'. Later on they may put them in sentences but use them wrongly, as in 'put cup in table', 'sit from chair'. One common mistake the children make is to confuse two words that are opposite in meaning, or else to use one word of the pair with its true and with its opposite meaning. Thus 'switch on light' may be a request to switch the light on or off depending on the circumstances. Often one can see that the child is using the word 'on' to say 'do something appropriate to the light' and that he has not grasped the precise meaning of 'on' and 'off'.

Words that usually occur in pairs are often confused. 'Brush' may be called 'comb', or 'sock' may be called 'shoe'. At first 'Mummy' and 'Daddy' may be misnamed. His general behaviour shows that this is not because the child does not know the difference. His problem is that he cannot call the proper word to mind quickly and easily and therefore he makes a verbal mistake.

The children may muddle the order of letters inside words, and may say 'accitt' for 'attic', 'diccifult' for 'difficult', 'pasghetti' for 'spaghetti'. The order of words in sentences may be reversed, for example 'put bed on blanket', 'have strawberry shake milk'. If you ask a child 'What will you put in the box?' he is quite likely to say 'cupboard', because he interprets what he hears as 'What will you put the box in?' Autistic children, even those few who make good progress in speaking, cannot use words flexibly, or to express subtle ideas. They tend to learn one meaning only for a word or a whole phrase, and stick to that. When the child first begins to understand, he hears his mother say 'Do you want a biscuit?' When he can speak, he too says 'Do you want a biscuit?' because that is the magic phrase which opens the biscuit tin. It sounds as if the child is calling himself 'you' instead of 'I'. (This is known technically as 'reversal of pronouns'.) Normal children may do this for a brief time but soon learn the proper use of pronouns. When you think about it it is not surprising that autistic children have these problems. The real mystery is how normal children learn to use the words correctly so quickly.

An autistic child may use a whole sentence to mean one thing only, because of the situation in which he first heard it. One child used to say 'Don't throw it out of the window' when he meant 'No'. The children tend to learn one name only for things, and therefore become confused if they hear, for example, the kitchen cooker called both a 'stove' and an 'oven'. It is easy to imagine their problems over words that can have two meanings, such as the noun 'sheet' (which might refer either to bed linen or to a piece of paper). If a mother says in conversation, 'I will meet you later on', her young autistic child may say 'Have meat dinner' with an expression of pleasure at having understood something at last.

The children have so little feeling for everyday speech that they can sound old-fashioned and pedantic, like the boy who said, 'May I extract a biscuit from the tin?' They tend to be literal and concrete. If asked 'What will you do when you get up from the table?' the answer is likely to be 'Stand on floor'. The speech of autistic children has been described as similar to that of a computer translating from a foreign language, and this does give an idea of the kinds of mistakes they tend to make.

iv *Poor pronunciation and voice control*

As I explained before, an autistic child may repeat phrases he hears from other people, with the correct pronunciation, accent and tone of voice that was used by the original speaker. When he tries to say things which he has thought out for himself his pronunciation may be very poor indeed. He has trouble with the same sounds that bother young normal children, such as 's' 'th' 'sh'. Autistic children often miss off the ends of words or use fragments of words – 'li' for 'lid' and 'bicle' for 'bicycle'. Some of them seem to have difficulty in distinguishing certain sounds they hear. They may confuse words that are rather similar, such as soup and soap, or else have trouble with telling the hard 'f' from the soft 'v' or the hard 'c' from the soft 'g'.

An autistic child usually has difficulty in controlling the volume of his voice. He finds it hard to produce a smooth flow of speech, his voice goes up and down in the wrong places, and may have a mechanical quality. Many children go through a phase in which they say some things in a 'special' voice, different from their ordinary one. This may be a copy of something they have heard, but sometimes seems to be an attempt to try out different sounds.

All these problems mean that the children have to make an effort to speak. They try to get round this by making sentences as short as they can. 'Home after bread' is a good example, meaning 'Let's go home after we have bought the bread'. Normal people use many more words than are strictly necessary, while autistic children are more economical.

v *Problems in understanding things that are seen*

Autistic children have just as many problems with understanding things they see as with things they hear. I have already described how, as babies, they ignore many things which normal children enjoy looking at, whereas they may be fascinated by lights or shiny metal or paper. This lasts into childhood. They may also be distressed by extra bright lights, such as those used for photography.

When young, the children may look at something that moves but lose interest when the movement stops. They seem to recognise people and objects by their general outline rather than by details of their appearance. This suggests that the children may make most use of the part of the eye which attends to movement and outline, and have problems in using the part which perceives fine detail. Normal people use the movement-detecting part mostly in conditions of near darkness, when it is not possible to observe any detail. It is therefore interesting that some autistic children walk downstairs and even ride a tricycle without seeming to look where they are going, and may find their way in the dark quite as easily as in the light. A number of parents have noticed that their young autistic child may not bother to switch on the light if alone in a dark room, but can find his possessions and move around with no difficulty. A group of psychologists have shown that autistic children, unlike normal children, do not fix their gaze on people or objects for any length of time, but dart rapid glances and then look away. This gives the impression that the children deliberately avoid looking at other people's faces, especially their eyes, but tests have shown that they look comparatively longer at human faces than they do at anything else. The exception to this is when they are fascinated by something such as a piece of shiny paper. Then they will gaze fixedly for long periods of time.

Many of the children are late in showing any interest in pictures. When they do begin to look at picture books, they tend to pick out one small piece of the whole, such as a bar of chocolate in a picture of a sweet shop, probably because they cannot take in the meaning of the whole scene. Very complicated and rapidly changing environments like crowded shops may upset a young autistic child, and bring on a temper tantrum.

vi *Problems in understanding gestures*

People can communicate with each other in many ways other than talking. They use gestures, facial expressions and bodily movements. In a foreign country they may mime their needs or demonstrate with objects. Deaf people can lip read, or use finger talk, or write down what they want to say. All these methods involve using one's eyes and understanding what is seen. Autistic children, unlike deaf children, are handicapped in using even these 'visual' languages. In the first year or so the only 'language' they have is indiscriminate screaming. In the stage after this, they show their needs by grabbing someone by the hand, pulling him along, and putting his hand on the desired object. It may be years before a child begins to point, and then he usually uses his whole hand and does not point one finger. The children are unable to mime. An autistic child does not ask for a drink by putting an imaginary cup to his lips and pretending to swallow. Often the children have to be taught to use such simple gestures as a smile or a hug to welcome their parents.

They have as much trouble in understanding visual languages as in using them. As time goes on, however, especially if they develop the ability to look at things for a longer time, and to be more aware of details, they begin to have some comprehension of the meaning of clear, simple gestures and expressions. Usually they make faster progress with understanding (though not with using) visual than with spoken language, and may then appear to understand more of what is said than they really do, because they find clues in people's faces and movements.

vii *The senses of touch, taste and smell*

Parents and teachers soon notice that autistic children explore the world through their senses of touch, taste and smell, and that they do this long after the baby and toddler stage has passed. They love the feel of smooth wood, plastic or soft fur. The children often seem to recognise other people through these senses, and may like to smell their parents' hands and explore their faces with a soft delicate touch like that of a blind child. They enjoy rough games involving physical contact, although sometimes they will pull away from a more gentle touch or a kiss.

Although willing to explore things by tasting them, some of the children have difficulty with learning to chew lumpy food, and have to have their food mashed up for them for considerably longer than normal. Young autistic children can appear insensitive to cold and pain. They will run out of doors with no clothes on in icy weather or ignore knocks and bumps. This usually becomes less marked with age and older children may be over-sensitive to discomfort. Some children, especially those in institutions where there is little occupation and supervision, may pick at sore places or injure themselves in various ways such as biting or head banging. These injuries may be severe although the child appears to feel no pain.

viii *Unusual bodily movements*

One of the most noticeable things about an autistic child is that he has many odd movements. He will flap his arms and hands, jump up and down, and make facial grimaces. He tends to walk on tiptoe, sometimes holding his legs stiffly. A few of the children spin round and round without becoming giddy. Nearly all of them twist and turn their fingers or objects near their eyes.

These movements of hands, limbs and face are most obvious when an autistic child is excited or is gazing at something which has absorbed his whole attention, such as a piece of string which he is twiddling in his fingers. On the other hand, if he is occupied in some constructive activity, the movements are hardly seen at all.

ix *Clumsiness in skilled movements*

One of the legends about autistic children is that they are graceful in movement. As usual, the facts are more complicated. Some autistic children are graceful when they walk, and are able to climb and balance like cats. Other children are rather clumsy and walk as if they have some difficulty in balancing, and they usually do not enjoy climbing.

The children may be skilful and nimble with their fingers, or they may be stiff and clumsy. A child who is good with his hands may be poorly co-ordinated in his walking and running, or vice versa. Any combination is possible.

However, nearly all autistic children, whether they appear to be graceful or clumsy, are immature in the way they move. They often hold their arms awkwardly when they run, even when they have reached the age when normal children run with elbows bent and arms held close to their sides. They may climb the stairs by standing on each step in turn, when they should be old enough to alternate one foot on each stair. They tend to be late in reaching the stage of steadily swinging the arms when walking.

Many of these children hold their arms in a special way when unoccupied. They have their elbows bent and their hands near together in front of them, drooping at the wrists, with fingers slightly curled.

It is also common to find that autistic children have problems when they try to copy movements made by other people, even when they reach the stage at which they are willing to co-operate. They may copy the reverse of the movement they see. That is, they will point down instead of up, and move the left arm instead of the right and so on. They usually cannot copy the movements of hopping on one foot, or skipping, and if they try an intricate dance step they become tangled up with their own feet.

This muddle about sequence and left-right, back-front and up-down affects many of their activities. I have already mentioned the tendency to mix the order of words in sentences. Some of the children, when they dress, tend to put clothes on back to front and shoes on the wrong feet. They lay the table with knives and forks on the wrong side and turn door handles in the wrong direction. If they begin to learn to read and write the letters of the alphabet, some autistic children confuse letters which are the reverse of each other, such as b and d, p and q, t and f, n and u and m and w.

DIFFICULT BEHAVIOUR AND EMOTIONAL PROBLEMS

Many people will feel that I should have started my description of autistic children with this section instead of putting it at the end. Behaviour difficulties are obvious and distressing in the early years, but there are good reasons, which I shall explain later, for believing that these problems follow from the children's inability to understand and cope with the world, and are not the first cause of their handicaps.

i *Aloofness and social withdrawal*

Most (though not all) young autistic children behave as though other people did not exist. It is possible to list the points in the behaviour of an autistic child which make him seem so aloof and distant – such a 'changeling child'. He does not come when he is called, he does not listen if you speak to him, his face may be empty of expression, he rarely looks straight at your face, he may pull away if you touch him, he does not put his arms round you if you pick him up, and he may walk past you (or over you, if you are sitting on the floor) without pausing in his stride. If he wants something he cannot reach for himself he grabs you by the back of your hand or wrist (not sliding his hand inside yours like a normal child) and pulls you along to do the work for him. Once he has the object you are ignored again. He shows no interest or sympathy if you are in pain or distress. He seems cut off, in a world of his own, completely absorbed in his own aimless activities.

However, the children do respond to adults who understand the handicaps and know how to break through the barriers these handicaps create. Then it is possible to see that the children have all the normal emotions, even if they are shown in very immature ways.

The children tend to become much more affectionate as they grow older. Sometimes when a child is five or six years old his mother feels that at last he is responding as he should have done when he was a baby.

ii *Resistance to change*

This problem may be shown in several different ways. Many of the children insist on repetition of the same routines. Paradoxically, when they are babies they may never settle to any routine of feeding or sleeping, but by the time they can walk they usually insist that certain things are done in precisely the same way every time. One child always wanted the same route for her daily walk, another insisted that the whole family kept to the same places at the table for every meal. A little boy would watch his mother lay the fire and become extremely upset if she did not place the paper, wood and coal in the same pattern every day. If the routine is upset there are screams and temper tantrums.

Some children have routines of their own, such as tapping on their chair before sitting down, standing up and turning round two or three times in the course of a meal, or placing objects in long lines.

Autistic children often become very attached to certain objects, and refuse to be parted from them. These may be ordinary toys like dolls or teddy bears, but often they are oddments such as pieces of string, holly leaves, tiny squares of photographic negative, or little bits of concrete. Some children are 'collectors' of such trifles as empty detergent packets, tins, plastic bottles, or dustpans. They will go to any lengths to add to their store. One little boy, when he realised he had to wait till detergent packets were empty, would throw away the powder from a full packet if it was left in his reach. Another child used to grab tins from displays in supermarkets, and would even run into people's houses to find old tins, if he was given the chance.

Resistance to change can apply to food, and though some autistic children have good appetites from the beginning, others go through a stage in which they refuse to eat more than two or three different things.

iii *Special fears*

It is quite common for the children to develop fears of harmless things, such as balloons, friendly dogs, or riding in buses. These fears can last for years, and may create difficulties for the whole family, especially if they are of common everyday objects or events which can hardly be avoided.

Conversely an autistic child can be unaware of real dangers, probably because he does not understand the possible consequences. One boy liked the sound of squealing car brakes and would dash in front of cars to make them brake sharply and thus produce this (to him) delightful noise.

Some autistic children are continually tense and frightened while others seem unconcerned and take things as they come. A child may change as he grows older, usually in the direction of becoming more relaxed. The differences are probably due to each child's own personality which determines the way he reacts to his handicaps.

iv *Socially embarrassing behaviour*

Since autistic children are limited in their understanding of words, and are generally immature, they often behave in ways which are socially unacceptable. Some of them are quiet and rather passive children and do not cause much trouble, but others are energetic and determined, and, especially in the years between two and five, their parents have to cope with an endless series of awful situations.

An autistic child who is given to screaming is not inhibited by being in a public place, and will scream as loud and long in the street as at home. He may take things off shop counters, run into the back premises of shops, or enter the homes of complete strangers. He has no idea that it is not done to take off one's clothes in public and will happily disrobe to sit in an inviting puddle of rain water, if so inclined. He will rub his face against a fur coat, and look right through the person wearing it if she speaks to him. His table manners may leave much to be desired, and most of the children will happily pick up any food they drop on the floor and eat it, regardless of any dirt that may be collected at the same time.

The children who learn to talk at least a little become much better behaved in general, but even they cause small social crises. They do not understand that some things are better left unsaid. They may talk about topics that are not mentioned in polite society. Innocently, they make remarks about other people which may be hurtful. One girl who spoke very well, on seeing an unusually short woman, said, in her loud, clear voice, 'Mummy, look at that *dear* little lady'. Just like young normal children, autistic children tend to pick up bad language and terms of abuse and bring them out on most unsuitable occasions.

Autistic children never tell lies. They do not understand why it should ever be necessary to avoid the truth, and in any case lack the skill with language and ideas needed to invent lies. Their naivety leads to a devastating lack of awareness of social conventions, or of other people's feelings.

v *Inability to play*

Normal children learn about the world through play. They begin by exploring the feel, taste and smell of different objects, but as they develop language and an understanding of the world around them they gradually begin to use toys to represent real things. They stop throwing the toy train on the floor to hear the noise it makes and start pretending that it will take them for a ride. They stop chewing the doll's foot and begin to cuddle it (the right way up), to dress it, to scold it – in short to pretend that the doll is a baby.

Autistic children have problems with all kinds of language, and their ability to play suffers in consequence. To them a toy train is not a pretence real train – it is just an object which is cold, hard, green, heavy, has a metallic taste and rattles when you shake it and makes funny patterns to look at when the wheels are spun. The children cxplore all objects, whether they are toys or discarded rubbish, in order to experience the simple sensations which give them great pleasure. As far as play is concerned, they remain at the stage of the baby who is just beginning to be able to hold things in his hands.

Most autistic children will play with water, sand or mud for hours on end (although a few of them have an intense dislike of becoming wet or dirty). They enjoy watching patterns of movement, and some become remarkably skilful at spinning coins or other objects. As they grow older, a number of the children are able to do jigsaws and similar puzzles, although they often fit the pieces by feel and not because of the clues from the pictures. They may also like constructional toys, although they are not really interested in the finished object but simply in the pleasure of fitting the pieces together.

Lacking language and imagination, they cannot join in other children's games. When young they ignore other children, but they may reach the stage when they want to take part but do not know how. Even the autistic children who have quite high intelligence are limited in their leisure activities. It is a common complaint of the parents of this kind of child that, although he is able to paint, or draw or play the piano, he has to be pushed into practising these skills, and seems to prefer unconstructive activity such as listening to the same record over and over again, or doing nothing at all.

SPECIAL SKILLS

So far, I have talked about autistic children's handicaps, but one of the surprising things is that some of them have special skills at which they perform well. This gives parents the feeling that their children would be completely normal if only the key to the puzzle could be found – if only something would 'make the penny drop'. Most of the children love music and rhythmic sounds. Some can sing well even at an early age, a few can play some musical instrument, and there are a smaller number still who are able to compose music.

The children can usually learn to use numbers more easily than words. Some of them are able to do long sums in their heads at great speed. They often like mechanical toys, and some learn to operate the radio and record player long before they learn to talk.

Many of the children are handicapped in drawing because of their problems with understanding the things they see. They draw strange-looking figures to represent human beings. Others who are more advanced may be able to draw and paint well, although they nearly always copy things they see or remember from the past, and are not creative.

Parents often notice that the children know at once if any of their special collections are disturbed in any way. They seem to recognise each pebble or piece of wood, even if to grown-up eyes one item is just like the other ninety-nine. The children may also be able to find their way back to places after one visit and know where objects of special interest (to them) are to be found in houses they have not visited for years.

None of these special abilities depends on language. Music, numbers, and memory for places are dealt with by different parts of the brain from those concerned with speech. There are stories about autistic children who could recite long poems or lists of names, but being able to learn like a parrot is not the same as being able to use language normally and fluently.

The general rule is that the children perform better at

skills which do not need language. These activities are their main source of enjoyment in life.

CHANGES AFTER FIVE YEARS OF AGE

Parents of autistic children have a hard time in the early years. The children's behaviour is so difficult, and progress seems so slow that their parents almost lose hope of any improvement. It is some comfort for them to know that, in general, there tends to be a distinct change for the better around five to seven years of age. This does not always happen. Some autistic children remain difficult, but the majority do improve at least to some extent after the first few years.

The biggest change is usually in the social and emotional problems. The children become more affectionate and sociable, less resistant to change, less given to needless fears but more aware of real danger, and better behaved in public. Their language problems and difficulties with movements also become less marked, but change in these areas is not so great as for general behaviour.

This improvement can create problems in diagnosis, since most writers describe autistic children as they are at their worst. When seeing older children, it is particularly important for the doctor to ask parents to give all the details they can about their child's behaviour in the early years.

ADOLESCENCE AND EARLY ADULT LIFE

Some autistic people go through this stage of life without any special problems, but in others there may be a number of difficulties. The more severely handicapped can become unco-operative and even aggressive. The mildly affected youngsters may continue to behave reasonably well but become sad, anxious or depressed as they begin to be aware of their handicaps. More follow-up studies are needed to show what is likely to happen in later adult life, but it appears from the evidence available so far that the problems of adolescence tend to settle down with increasing maturity.

5

Theories of causes

There are, in general, two main kinds of theories. One says that autistic children are normal when they are born, but that their emotional development is disturbed because of the way they are brought up. A special variant of this is that autistic children have the wrong kind of learning experiences from the time they are born, and are 'conditioned' into abnormal behaviour.

The other kind of theory suggests that autistic children have some physical abnormality in their brain that makes them behave in the way they do.

Parents, quite naturally, are inclined to resent the emotional theories, because however carefully the explanations are worded, the parents feel they are being blamed. Indignation and a refusal to be browbeaten into guilt are healthy reactions, but it is also necessary to consider the evidence as carefully as possible and to understand the basis for these ideas.

THEORIES SUGGESTING EMOTIONAL CAUSES

Kanner believed the social aloofness and indifference of the classically autistic child was the primary problem leading to all the other abnormalities. He wrote that the fathers of the children he saw were almost all high achievers, but odd, over-intellectual, rigid, detached, humourless – dedicated to their professions rather than to their families. He suggested that early childhood autism might be due to the inheritance of the father's social remoteness in very marked form, or the result of peculiar child-rearing practices of abnormal parents, or a combination of both these problems.

Later writers also put forward theories related to abnormalities in the relationship between parents and children, though they differed on the exact nature of the abnormalities concerned.

All these theories concerning the parents of autistic children were based on the writers' personal impressions, which could easily have been biased. In recent years there have been a number of studies which have used more objective methods to compare groups of parents of autistic children with those of other handicapped and normal children. The use of other types of handicaps as a comparison is particularly important, since having a handicapped child is likely to give rise to emotional reactions in anyone. These studies produced no evidence that parents of autistic children were especially abnormal in personality or in child-rearing practices.

The unsolved controversy as to the intelligence level and occupation of parents of typically autistic children was mentioned in Chapter 4. Even if their occupational class is higher than average, there is no reason to assume that this is related to abnormality in the parent-child relationship. Furthermore, while it is possible for parents to have more than one autistic child, in most cases the brothers and sisters are healthy and normal.

Finally, no one has ever shown that orphanages or institutions which give no mothering to the babies, and where the staff have no time to talk to the children, produce autistic children, although they may well have other kinds of undesirable effects in the short or long term.

The evidence that has accumulated against a primarily emotional cause for autism shows how wrong it is to rely entirely upon subjective judgements without proper methods of measurement. It is hard for parents that the early theories of parental abnormality were put forward without any scientific proof, and have caused much unhappiness ever since.

THEORIES SUGGESTING PHYSICAL CAUSES

The weight of the evidence is now on the side of a physical (also called an 'organic') cause for early childhood autism and related conditions.

Research work on organic factors is being carried out at three different, but inter-related, levels. The first concerns the basic causes of the possible brain pathology. A variety of conditions can lead to autistic behaviour, and such causes can be identified in more than one-third of the affected children. They include, among others, encephalitis (infection of the brain) in the early years of life, rubella (German measles) in the mother during pregnancy, untreated phenylketonuria (a biochemical abnormality that can be treated with a special diet if diagnosed in infancy), tuberose sclerosis (an inherited condition giving small patches of abnormal tissue in the brain and skin), infantile spasms (a rare and severe form of epilepsy occurring in the first year of life) and severe complications during birth, including lack of oxygen. Children who are born with severe visual problems and brain damage are very likely to show autistic features.

A study of twins has produced the theory that some cases of early childhood autism are due to an inherited factor. In other cases, the child may inherit a language problem, but develops autism only if he has additional brain damage due, for example, to a difficult birth. Finally, in yet other cases, the autism is due entirely to non-inherited organic factors operating before, during or after birth.

When considering basic causes, it is interesting to note that children with Down's syndrome, although their brains are markedly abnormal in development, are usually not autistic unless they have some other organic condition to complicate the picture.

Although clear organic causes can be found in a substantial minority of autistic children, there remain many where the reason is not known, especially among those who are only mildly handicapped.

The second level of research concerns how and where the basic causes operate in the brain. Does the inherited factor or the pre-, peri- or post-natal injury or illness affect the brain directly or indirectly, perhaps through some abnormality of the body's chemistry? Which aspect of the brain's structure or function has to be damaged or impeded in its development for autistic behaviour to occur? All kinds of theories have been put forward, and many parts of the brain considered as the essential site – including the reticular system, the dominant cortical hemisphere and the basal ganglia – but no one has yet produced any convincing proof. If the answers are to be found, work on the structure and functions of the normal human brain is just as important as investigations of pathology in people known to be autistic. Advances in both fields may follow from the development of new methods for examining the central nervous system.

The third level on which research is taking place concerns the nature of the psychological functions which are impaired as a result of the brain malfunction. It has been suggested that the children cannot attend to relevant events in the environment because they are in a continual state of excitement (over-arousal), but this has never been proved. It seems clear that impairments of understanding and use of language are an important aspect of autism and related conditions, but the problem is to define the abnormalities.

Difficulty in understanding and using speech is not a sufficient explanation, since there are children with such handicaps, suffering from developmental receptive speech disorders, who can understand and use *non-verbal* communication and who are not autistic.

The impairment of language in autism involves non-verbal as well as verbal communication, so is more severe and global than that in the developmental speech disorders (once known as congenital aphasias). But there are children with no speech and no symbolic gestures who are not autistic. These are normal babies under one year of age, and very severely retarded but non-autistic children. The essential difference is that the normal baby and even the non-autistic retarded child is interested in the new experiences that come to him, and is especially alert and pleased when approached by other human beings. He tries to communicate with facial expressions, noises and bodily movements long before the development of speech.

It is this curiosity and interest in new experiences, and the recognition of and desire to communicate with other humans that seems to be lacking in the autistic child. It seems that he can find little or no meaning in his world, and therefore has no basis for thinking, imagining and communicating his thoughts to other people. If he does learn, it is by rote. Even if he develops speech, he says as little as possible or else repeats the same things over and over again with little or no variation. Most baffling of all to the autistic person are the social rules which, by comparison, non-autistic children learn so easily from experience, mostly without specific teaching.

Just how the non-autistic brain operates to give meaning to experience, and how impairment of this ability relates to all the other aspects of autistic behaviour remains to be investigated. All that can be claimed for this formulation is that it does emphasise a very important aspect of autistic conditions.

Presumably the autistic children who have a high level of skill in areas not involving meaning and imagination have the pathology underlying autism and no other handicaps. Those with lower levels of skill, or no abilities at all, probably have the autistic pathology as part of a wider picture of brain damage or dysfunction. Conversely, it can be suggested that non-autistic retarded children have a variety of problems affecting brain structure and function, but not involving those essential for producing autistic behaviour.

Considering the wide range of autistic and autistic-like conditions, it seems likely that there will be a number of sub-groups with different causes and basic impairments, though with aspects in common. Perhaps the group described by Kanner will prove to be special in some way, but this remains to be seen.

6

Comparisons with other childhood handicaps and problems

DIFFICULT PHASES IN NORMAL CHILDREN

Everything that an autistic child does, normal children may do at some time or other during their development. Normal children have problems while learning to talk and to read and write; they sometimes take no notice when spoken to; they may ignore other people; they have temper tantrums; they may hold on to a piece of rag or a teddy bear and weep when it is lost; they have their special fears, and they sometimes seem oblivious of danger. The difference is that in a normal child these things happen in passing phases, whereas they continue for years on end in an autistic child. Also, normal children have imagination and widely varied activities, while autistic children are limited and repetitive in the things they do. When they are seen together, the contrast between a normal and an autistic child is painfully obvious.

CONGENITAL DEAFNESS

Children who are born deaf have many problems in learning to understand and use spoken language. They may be socially withdrawn and difficult in their behaviour and have various symptoms seen in autistic children, especially when young. However, they are able to learn gestures, miming, lip-reading and finger language. They use their eyes in communication, and they develop pretend play.

It is important to make sure that children with autistic

behaviour are not deaf. Testing is often a difficult problem, but the parents' observations of their child's behaviour at home can be most helpful in making a decision.

As explained in the previous section, some children born both deaf and blind behave like autistic children. The diagnosis depends on the history and physical examination.

DEVELOPMENTAL SPEECH DISORDERS

Children with these difficulties have problems with spoken language. Those with the receptive form have severe difficulty in understanding words, and therefore in learning to speak. Those with expressive problems can understand reasonably well but have difficulty in producing words for themselves. The children with receptive abnormalities are very likely to be confused with autistic children when young because they too tend to ignore sounds and to be socially withdrawn. The children with the expressive disorders are more responsive and sociable but they have the same problem as autistic children in copying movements made by other people and in speaking. Children with these conditions differ from autistic children in that they use their eyes to help them understand the world, and they communicate well in non-verbal ways. They also have pretend play.

It is possible to find some children with speech disorders who are very similar to autistic children. Receptive and expressive problems can occur in association with early childhood autism. The conditions all shade into each other and it is often hard to tell in which group to place a particular child. A description of each child's handicaps is therefore more use than giving him a single diagnostic label.

VISUAL PROBLEMS

Children may have visual problems because of conditions affecting the eyes, or the nerves from the eyes to the brain, or the parts of the brain receiving messages from the eyes. Sometimes, depending on the cause and the nature of the handicap, children with visual problems may have the same kinds of hand movements, and the same tendency to jump and spin round as autistic children. They may even be very concerned about routines and become most unhappy if anything in the house is moved from its usual place. They may appear to look past or through other people, and their social behaviour may be a problem. It is usually possible to tell the difference between autistic children and children with visual problems alone, because the latter do not have the same difficulties with understanding the things they hear. The history and physical examination also give the diagnosis.

MENTAL RETARDATION

This is a general label covering a large number of syndromes and behaviour patterns. It may result from a wide variety of inherited or acquired conditions affecting intellectual development, including those listed in Chapter 5 that may be associated with autism. As explained in that chapter, autism and mental retardation may occur together or independently. Among children who are severely retarded, a substantial minority have autism or autistic features. The autistic behaviour pattern can be found in the mildly retarded, but is much less common.

Non-autistic retarded children, especially those who are severely handicapped, are likely to have language problems, but they differ from autistic children in that they seek and enjoy social interaction for its own sake and not just for the gratification of some physical need. If they understand language at least as well as a nineteen- or twenty-month-old normal child, they will use some gestures to communicate and will have some pretend play. The questions to be asked in diagnosis are not 'Is this child autistic *or* is he mentally retarded?' but 'Is he autistic, *and* what is his level of intellectual function?' They can be answered only by careful observation of behaviour and testing the child's level of skill in non-verbal and verbal tasks.

ELECTIVE MUTISM

A very small number of children talk in one situation (for example at home) but remain silent elsewhere (for example at school). This is fairly common in toddlers when first beginning to speak, but if it goes on until school age it is a cause for concern. Children with 'elective mutism', as it is called, may have a variety of speech and behaviour problems, but the pattern of their behaviour is different from that of an autistic child. The diagnosis has to be made by considering all the symptoms together, and not just the fact that the child is silent in some places. One of the most important distinguishing features is that the child with elective mutism can use speech and gestures fairly fluently when he does talk, and does not have the kind of speech disorders that occur in childhood autism.

TYPES OF CHILDHOOD PSYCHOSIS

The differences between the early childhood psychoses, in which autistic features predominate, and the adult psychoses occurring in children, which begin after five years of age, have already been mentioned (see footnote on page 14). The diagnosis is made on the child's history, and present behaviour pattern.

Various ways of sub-grouping the early childhood psychoses have been suggested, including defining typical Kanner's syndrome as a special group. This is of interest to research workers attempting to find causes and define the nature of the handicaps. From the point of view of education, management of behaviour and prediction of future progress, a classification based on the level of practical skill, and the level of development of language and imagination, however limited, is the most useful.

EFFECTS OF DEPRIVATION

Babies and young children who are seriously deprived of stimulating experiences, especially close contact and communication with a caring person, are held back in social, language and intellectual development. They may be so withdrawn and unresponsive that they give the impression of being autistic. Careful observation of the full behaviour pattern shows the differences, but the most important point for diagnosis is the effect of providing the child with better care and wider experiences. The deprived child, within a few weeks or even days of being given such care, begins to make great strides in his development in all areas. The autistic child's progress, on the other hand, is painfully slow and his basic handicaps remain, even after years of loving care and patient teaching.

Clarke and Clarke, in their book *Early Experience: Myths and Evidence*, give some most interesting examples of deprived children who were eventually rescued, and discuss the unsolved question as to how long severe deprivation has to continue before the effects on the child become irreversible.

Difficulties in diagnosis arise if a child who is mentally retarded or autistic also happens to be deprived in his early years. The temptation is to explain the handicaps as resulting from the poor environment, but a careful consideration of all the evidence shows the inappropriateness of this type of explanation, even in an individual case.

Part II
Education and management

Autistic children's handicaps are severe, they affect all the activities of daily living, and they are usually lifelong, though tending to a slow improvement. There is no known cure for these handicaps, but this does not mean that nothing can be done. The children can be helped to find ways round their difficulties with special methods of education, both at home and at school. In many ways the problem is similar to that faced by the parents and teachers of deaf or blind children. It may not be possible to cure the handicaps, but the children can be taught to make the best use of the skills they do possess. Some of the children have too many additional handicaps to make much progress, but even in these cases it is worth trying to improve the worst behaviour problems and to teach simple self-care.

7

What doctors can do

When parents first realise that there is something wrong with their child, they desperately hope that doctors will be able to make him better. They go to their first appointment with high expectations, which are bound to be disappointed. Sometimes they feel anger and bitterness against the doctor himself, and perhaps seek advice from one clinic after another. This is a waste of time and may even be harmful for the family if the parents never come to terms with reality. The problem is made worse by the fact that parents are likely to meet many different theories on their travels, and they become confused and depressed. Occasionally they even meet with professional workers who at first believe that they can *cure* the child with psychological treatment. After a varying period of time it becomes obvious that this is not going to happen. The therapist may decide to discontinue the treatment, and the parents feel let down, and that their child has been rejected once again.

It requires considerable courage for parents to make their own decision as to whom to trust and whose advice to follow. They usually have to make such a decision on the grounds of their own common sense and experience with children. They are fortunate if they can meet a number of other parents of older autistic children and find out for themselves which ideas have proved useful.

Doctors and parents can work together best if parents have reasonable expectations of how much the doctor can do.

DIAGNOSIS

Making sure of the diagnosis is the doctor's first task. He has to study the child's past history and behaviour and decide how far the pattern fits that of early childhood autism. He then goes on to find out if the child has any of the conditions which can be mistaken for autism. In particular he has to satisfy himself that the child is not deaf, and has no difficulty with seeing.

The next step is to consider if the child has any associated handicaps. These might be abnormalities of the brain and nervous system such as spasticity or fits, or he might have some other physical problem which adds to his difficulties. Doctors have to be especially careful in assessing these extra handicaps, because the child cannot complain for himself and his odd behaviour might hide symptoms and signs that would be obvious in a normal child.

A detailed diagnosis takes time, and needs trust and co-operation between the doctor and his assistants on the one side, and the family on the other.

DISCUSSION WITH PARENTS

I have put this near the top of the list of the things that doctors can do, because a full and frank discussion as soon as possible after the parents realise that the child is handicapped can have a positive effect upon their whole attitude to the problem in the future.

Most parents like to be given a name for what is wrong with their child, but the sensible doctor does not leave it at that. He can explain to the parents how their child is handicapped. For example he can tell them that their little boy can understand simple instructions but not complicated ones, and that he has problems in pronunciation. He can let the parents know about the child's difficulties in comprehending the things he sees, and how all these handicaps upset his emotions and his behaviour. A detailed analysis of this kind is much more helpful than giving the child a label.

The parents also want to know about the prospects for the future. They will appreciate it if they are told the truth. They need to know that the handicaps are long-lasting, but also that they, as parents, can do an enormous amount to help their child if they set about it in the right way.

It is a hard task for a doctor to have to tell parents that they have a severely handicapped child. A doctor in this situation has to deal with his own emotions as well as those of the parents, and it requires all his skill, experience, and human compassion to handle the situation successfully, and to build a basis for a co-operative effort throughout the long years ahead.

TREATMENT OF ADDITIONAL HANDICAPS

The more handicaps a child has, the harder he finds it to cope with life. It is therefore important to make sure that an autistic child is as physically fit as possible. Sometimes it is difficult to give special treatment when the child is young (such as exercises for spasticity, or glasses for poor vision) but efforts can be made at intervals, and the full procedures started as soon as he is at the stage when he can co-operate, or at least not fight against the efforts to help him.

Routine physical care, such as inoculations, dental care, and treatment for childish illnesses, is often a problem. Suggestions for parents will be given in the next section, but doctors and dentists can do their work more effectively if they get to know the child and obtain his trust before he needs any medical or dental care.

Having to wait a long time to be seen is a strain for a handicapped child. It is also hard on the parents and the other patients if the child's behaviour becomes disturbed. The understanding doctor or dentist tries to arrange appointments to avoid this problem, if the circumstances make this possible.

ALLEVIATION OF SECONDARY BEHAVIOUR PROBLEMS

Medical methods are sometimes useful for relieving special problems. One example is sleeplessness, especially when the child keeps the whole family awake every night because of his screaming. If nothing else works, the doctor may prescribe sleeping tablets as a temporary measure. Tablets of this kind must never be given without a doctor's advice. This is a good rule, but it is particularly important where autistic children are concerned. They may be resistant to normal doses of sedatives, and sometimes drugs can excite a child instead of calming him down.

Overactivity and restlessness can sometimes be helped by drugs prescribed by a doctor. In general it is better to try to improve the child's behaviour through sensible management, because drugs have undesirable side effects and in any case may not produce the desired result. There are times, however, when medication has to be tried.

HELP WITH PLANNING AN EDUCATIONAL PROGRAMME

Doctors can help parents and teachers to plan a programme of education by telling them the details of the child's handicaps. Examples of ways in which this knowledge can be used will be given in the next sections.

Passing on information should be a continuing and a two-way process. Parents and teachers are with the children for many hours each day and are in a position to observe behaviour that a doctor can never see in a brief office visit. Evaluation of the child's handicaps and the progress he is making can be done most effectively if all the available information is brought together in regular discussions.

PSYCHOTHERAPY

Psychotherapy and even psychoanalysis have been attempted with autistic children, but there is no evidence that they are effective in curing or even diminishing the children's handicaps. This is not surprising since psychotherapeutic techniques presuppose the development of language and the ability to symbolise, and these are the skills which autistic children conspicuously lack. The use of psychotherapeutic techniques which encourage 'regression' (for example, bottle feeding a child of seven to encourage him to go back to the baby stage and 'start again') seems particularly inappropriate for autistic children. The theory is that the child has to be returned to the stage before his development went wrong, and that he will then be able to 'begin again' and will develop normally. However there is no scientific evidence that these techniques are helpful. The most successful methods are those which try to help the child move forward in development, rather than backward. Sometimes older children who have made good progress and who are able to talk fairly well become unhappily aware that they are different from others of their age. Such a child could be helped by psychotherapy from someone who understood his handicaps. Autistic children, like normal children, may be depressed by the loss of someone they love and depend upon, and by other major crises of life, and may need the help of someone experienced in this kind of work.

Professional workers who hold theories which imply that the parents 'cause' their child to become autistic may recommend that these parents should have psychotherapy or psychoanalysis, in order to help the child indirectly. There is no evidence that this is useful in practice.

On the whole parents find that their emotional distress is lessened as they begin to understand what is wrong with their child, and, even more important, what they can do to help him. Some families find they can accept a handicapped child fairly easily, and come to terms with their unhappiness as time goes on. Others are less philosophical, for many different personal reasons. Some of these parents may want and benefit from psychotherapy given by someone who understands what it means to have a child who is different. The aim should be to lessen any tendency to morbid self-blame, and release the parents' energies for the task in hand.

8

What teachers can do

This book is written for parents, and is not intended to give details of methods of education. All I shall do is to mention the important role which teachers play in helping autistic children to achieve their full potential.

A teacher's task is easier if an autistic child has reasonable social behaviour, if he can feed, wash and dress himself and is clean and dry in the day time, but she often has to begin by teaching these skills.

Once this basic behaviour has been established, the teacher can go on to other things. Teaching methods have to be adapted to the children's handicaps, and use many of the techniques for blindness, deafness and speech disorders. Montessori equipment is good because much of it gives the children the opportunity of using touch and movement for learning. All the ways of teaching I shall mention in the next section are used in specialist schools – that is, teaching motor skills by guiding the child's limbs, helping learning by the proper use of encouragement and discouragement, and, for the more advanced children, the use of pictures, diagrams and models to get across an idea without depending solely upon words.

The subjects taught in special schools include those which can be found in the normal school curriculum such as reading, writing, arithmetic, music, art, cooking, sewing and other domestic work, wood work and metal work. The difference is that most schools for autistic children cater for a wide range of abilities, so some children will be able to achieve only a few simple skills, while a few can move on to wider subjects. The majority, somewhere between the two ends of the scale, are very handicapped in learning, but their school experience improves their ability to cope with life. Good teachers know from experience when to watch and wait, and when to apply some pressure to ensure that a child moves forward in learning. They know how to make the best use of the improvement which occurs as a child grows and matures so that no opportunity is lost. One important aspect of school is that it provides a structured environment and experience of social mixing. School outings, birthday and Christmas parties and the daily assembly of the whole school, give a rhythm and pattern to life which the children find both comforting and stimulating. The most successful schools, once they are well established, develop a tradition of reasonable behaviour which is a great asset. Even the most disturbed children become calmer and more co-operative when introduced into such an atmosphere. Teachers find that autistic children are considerably influenced by these social pressures, even though they appear to ignore the other children. It is impressive to observe the social competence that can be acquired in the right kind of school. Children who appeared confused and lost can learn to find their way around the school with confidence, and carry out all the small routines with calm assurance.

A teacher is one member of the team which should be concerned in helping an autistic child. She has to work with doctors and psychologists, as a professional with her own expertise, but willing to use the knowledge and advice provided by experts in other fields. She needs to have knowledge and experience of normal child development and of teaching normal children, so that she can recognise the stages in the progress of an autistic child, and not mistake immature behaviour for a pathological symptom. She is also an important person for the parents. She can learn a lot about the children in her care by listening to the parents' account of the behaviour at home. Methods of management which have been found to work at school and at home can be exchanged, and problems and possible solutions discussed. A parent-teacher association provides an excellent opportunity for co-operation between home and school. A teacher is sometimes in a particularly good position to help parents who have lost heart, and who do not know how to help their own child. If the teacher can help him to make progress the parents may be able to find fresh courage and to learn from her success.

One thing that teachers and parents have to avoid is jealousy over who can manage the child best. Both home and school play their own special parts in the plan for helping the child. The roles are different but complementary and both are of equal value. Problems can also arise if teachers try to assume the role of psychotherapists for the child, the parents or the whole family. The teachers' real skills are too important to be hampered by attempting to mix them with those of a different discipline.

Autistic adolescents, especially those who have made only slow progress in school work, can present special problems to a teacher. There is a tendency to continue with the same simple work that has been performed in childhood. But an adolescent can become very bored with tasks he was willing to do as a child, and this may add to the behaviour problems that tend to occur around this stage of life. Teachers need to be aware of this possibility and plan to change the content of the teaching programme, so that it is more acceptable to someone who, even though he is handicapped, is becoming an adult.

9

What parents can do

AUTISTIC BABIES

Autism is usually not diagnosed until the age of two or later, so no one can recommend well-tried and -tested ways of dealing with problems in babies who are going to be autistic children. Parents usually look back regretfully to the early days, and think how much better they would have managed if only they had understood what was wrong.

SOCIAL INTERACTION

It seems reasonable to suggest that, if a baby seems unresponsive, his mother should make a special effort to cuddle him, tickle, him, carry him around and talk to him, so that he has the same experiences as a normal baby. The relationship between a mother and a normal baby is built up by each responding to the other. The baby depends on his mother to play with him and caress him, so that he can learn to be sociable and come to realise how important she is to him. On the other hand, a mother needs her baby to show his pleasure in her company, by cooing, chuckling, wriggling with delight and making himself ready to be picked up. An autistic baby who seems aloof and self-contained misses out on these vital early interactions with his mother, not because she is abnormal, but because he is handicapped.

A mother with this kind of baby has to be encouraged to do all the work herself, and she is usually only too happy to do this, once she realises that she will not harm the baby by breaking into his isolation.

BABY TALK

The baby's lack of interest in his mother's baby-talk tends to make her talk less and less, until she says as little to him as he does to her. Again, explanation and encouragement are needed so that she chats to the baby even if he takes no notice. Many mothers remember that their autistic children liked having words whispered right into their ear. This makes sense, because experts in the way children develop language point out that babies learn to talk on their mothers' laps, hearing their mothers' voices while in close physical contact. Whispering into the baby's ear brings mother and child even closer, and adds pleasant physical sensations as well.

Another way of getting an autistic child's attention is to sing to him. Baby talk and simple sentences can be sung to tunes he likes, and his first word may be the last word of the line of a nursery rhyme.

SLEEPLESSNESS AND SCREAMING

If the baby screams regularly every night for some hours, it may be helpful for the parents to arrange between them to have one night looking after the baby and one night sleeping. Loss of sleep can be extremely wearing, and help from a relative or a children's nurse may be the only solution to give the parents a few nights' unbroken sleep. It is important that the child should meet a new night-nurse in his mother's company, and in the day time before she takes charge for the night. If this is not arranged, the sudden appearance of a stranger can make the child even more disturbed than usual.

It is worth while trying different ideas to see if a sleepless screaming baby can be helped to settle. Some babies like to have a light left on. One little boy would sleep peacefully only if he were wrapped up tightly in a sheet, like a little cocoon. The old-fashioned remedy of rocking sometimes works. A few parents have had to give their baby sedatives, under the supervision of a doctor, since this was the only way to break a habit of sleepless nights which had gone on for many months.

AUTISTIC CHILDREN

Once babyhood has passed, and the child can walk, the pattern of autistic behaviour becomes obvious. The diagnosis is usually made around this time, and parents have to begin the long process of helping their child to fit into the family and the world. The problems they meet during the years of childhood are many and varied, and each child has his own special difficulties as well as those which are common to most of the children. All I can do here is to write about some of the situations with which parents have to cope, and to make some suggestions based on ideas which have proven helpful in practice.

In the early years when the children have few, if any, means of communication, the management of difficult behaviour is the first priority. Later on, as communication develops, behaviour is less difficult, and the main problems are teaching the skills of living and trying to stimulate the children's interest in constructive activities.

MANAGING DIFFICULT BEHAVIOUR

Having a disturbed child makes most people feel that they are miserable failures as parents, even though the other children in the family may behave quite normally. The thing to remember is that the ordinary methods of bringing up children, based largely on the supposition that the child understands what you say to him, do not work with autistic children. Parents cannot help making mistakes because they naturally act towards the child as if he were normal, right up until the time when they begin to understand why he is so different.

In general, parents and teachers need to discourage disturbed behaviour and to encourage constructive, socially acceptable behaviour. Normal babies and children learn in a number of different ways. Firstly, early on, they become aware of their mother's tone of voice, the expression on her face, small nods or shakes of her head, the way she stands and moves, all of which show whether she is approving or disapproving. Secondly, as soon as they begin to understand the words they hear, normal children can learn through speech as well as gestures. Thirdly, they also imitate their parents as best they can within the limits of their understanding.

None of these ways is particularly rapid or efficient in the very young child, because his capacity to understand has to grow and mature, so in an emergency a parent has to use a more direct method of teaching. If a baby crawls towards a boiling kettle, his mother does not rely on gestures, words, or his ability to imitate in order to prevent an accident. Instead, she grabs him as soon as she realises what he intends to do, and she continues to prevent him from scalding himself even if he becomes annoyed and tearful. Similarly a mother instinctively uses direct physical methods (such as hugging and kissing) to show her approval when her baby has done something which pleases her. She knows that words and gestures are not enough by themselves, although she uses them as well.

The problem with a young autistic child is that the first three ways of learning are closed to him because of his language handicaps, and only the last way is available. With the development of language, normal children begin to be able to remember and to anticipate. They can understand if they are warned not to behave in a certain way, and if they are scolded after they have been naughty. As they mature, this capacity to look both backward and forward in time increases, until finally a normal adult can plan for years in the future. Autistic children, until they develop some ability to communicate, are bound by the present. They link things that happen at the same time, or very close in time, whether this is justified or not, and they are unable to appreciate the connection between two events which are a few minutes apart. It is all too easy for these children to make mistakes about how things link together, as I shall describe in the discussion of 'special fears'.

Recently, a number of psychologists have become interested in the direct methods of learning which are useful with children and adults with limited comprehension of language. The techniques they have developed are known as 'operant conditioning' or 'behaviour modification'. These methods have been discussed widely in the popular press as well as in scientific journals, and sometimes they have received adverse publicity and strong criticism. This is firstly because some workers have used harsh ways of discouraging undesirable behaviour; secondly because 'conditioning' appears to mean a detached, scientific approach to bringing up children; and thirdly because of the possibility that behaviour learnt under special concentrated conditions may not generalise to everyday life in the school, or at home with the family.

These objections are still being debated in the scientific literature on learning theory. However, some of the basic principles are accepted by almost everyone, and fit well into a general programme of child-rearing and education. Parents and teachers can borrow the most useful techniques from the specialists, and apply them to suit their own children. In a few places, mostly in the USA, professional workers provide special teaching for parents to enable them to help their children in their own homes. This most promising idea is beginning to arouse interest in many centres concerned with handicapped children. It is worth noting that people who are intuitively good with children have always made use of many of the ideas which the psychologists have had to work out from long laborious studies.

The first step is to try to understand why a child behaves in a particular way. It is helpful to remember that the behaviour of an autistic child, though it often appears to be bizarre and strange, always has a concrete logical reason behind it. By this, I mean that it is the simple response of a handicapped child faced with a complex situation which he does not understand. Is is not the expression of inner fantasies, because these depend on the comprehension and use of some kind of symbolic language.

The studies of methods of changing behaviour have confirmed the obvious, in that they have shown that children tend to repeat behaviour which in the past has led to reward, and to stop behaving in ways that are not rewarded.

When dealing with a child who cannot speak and who cannot understand very much, it is vital to time things so that you react *at once* to reward or to discourage. The best thing is to act to prevent bad behaviour, or if that cannot be done, to take action as soon as the behaviour starts. This is more likely to work than allowing a child to do something naughty or dangerous, and then punishing him afterwards. It seems that if he has already had the fun of doing the forbidden act, the punishment counts for little. Many parents find that their child is not deterred by being smacked after he has done something wrong. He may even laugh, or cheerfully anticipate the slap as a routine consequence of certain actions. Psychologists say that in this situation the slap acts, in a curious way, as a reward. Another problem is that children with poor comprehension of speech easily become confused about the reasons why their parents show disapproval. If you threaten to 'tell Daddy when he comes home', the child will have completely forgotten the reason a few moments later, and all he will learn is that Daddy is a person who often becomes very cross when he arrives home. This will make him unhappy about his father but will have no effect at all on his difficult behaviour.

To be effective, you must act quickly *every time* the child begins to show the difficult behaviour. The mother in the example of the boiling kettle knows that she has to prevent her baby reaching the kettle whenever the problem recurs. After a time he gets the message that, try as he might, the kettle is forbidden.

The way you respond should be easily understood by the child. Trying to prevent an autistic child from breaking a window by talking to him has no effect. Shouting at him may put him off at first, but he will become accustomed to that after a time. If you become angry after the window is broken, and show it very obviously, this may have the opposite effect to that which you intended. A young autistic child who does not understand the implications of the signs of rage may feel that an angry parent is an interesting and exciting event, and he will therefore be encouraged rather than deterred. This is particularly likely to happen if he is left alone when quiet, but becomes the centre of attention when he creates a disturbance. As with the baby and the kettle, it is more effective to take action to hold him and remove him before the window is broken. This has the advantage that it can be turned into a cuddle, or a tickling game, or whatever you know the child enjoys. Sometimes parents give up trying because they find that their child does not respond to their efforts to control his behaviour. This is usually because they try methods which they expect to work with a normal child, but which are meaningless to an autistic child. In this situation the parents have to be encouraged to observe as carefully as they can in order to find their own child's likes and dislikes, and then to work out a programme which will be effective in practice.

Certain kinds of behaviour cannot be anticipated or prevented. A good example is a sudden outburst of screaming for no obvious reason. Then the best method is to ignore the child, and only to attend to him when he stops doing the thing you wish to prevent. In this case, you are rewarding him through your interest and attention, a reward which he receives only when he is not indulging in the undesirable behaviour.

It is an important principle that if you want to improve a child's general behaviour you should help him find positive, constructive things to do. It is no good stopping him spending his time hitting his head against a wall, if the only alternative is to sit in a chair with no occupation at all. In these circumstances the head banging is likely to start up again.

If you sometimes prevent a problem and at other times overlook it, this seems to have a worse effect than taking no action at all. This is one example of the general finding that an inconsistent approach creates even more difficulties than over-strictness or over-permissiveness. However, consistency is difficult to achieve, particularly for a busy mother with more than one child needing her attention. For this reason it is best to decide to take a firm stand on the most important behaviour problems, but to leave the ones which are not particularly inconvenient. This compromise results in a reasonably relaxed atmosphere, but also allows the child to learn that there are limits beyond which he may not go.

The best teaching techniques in the world are no use unless they are used by someone who really loves the child concerned and has his best interests at heart. Success depends upon knowing the child, understanding his handicaps, being aware of his likes and dislikes, and being able to guess what he intends to do before he starts to do it. These insights are almost impossible to achieve in the absence of any positive feeling for the child.

i *Screaming and temper tantrums*

(The suggestions in this section apply to fits of screaming and temper tantrums which occur as part of a pattern of disturbed behaviour. They are not appropriate for screaming brought on by physical illness, or pain, or some other understandable reason. In these situations the cause has to be found and dealt with. It is not always possible to distinguish the reasons for tantrums, but parents have to rely on their experience of their own child and make the best guess they can.)

Young autistic children often have tantrums because they have no words with which to ask for the things they want. They may scream in order to obtain sweets, cakes or ice-creams, or for some oddment which interests them at the time, or because a routine has been disturbed. Parents, being only human, tend to deal with the situation by giving the child something to soothe and quieten him because they know from bitter experience that the screams can go on for hours. Unfortunately, the child, being only human too, soon 'learns' that the quickest way of getting anything he wants is to scream and shout and stamp and kick – in short to have a first-class temper tantrum. He does not work this out in words, but he learns through his own and his parents' actions.

The way to prevent, rather than to encourage, tantrums is to make sure that the child is never given the things he wants while he is actually showing this behaviour. This requires courage and determination because the policy must be put into practice in public, as well as at home. If a child has a tantrum in the street or in a shop, the only solution may be to remove him from the scene as rapidly as possible.

When at home, the child should be ignored while he is screaming. It may be possible to put him in another room away from the rest of the family, but only if he can come to no harm and do no damage while by himself. The moment the tantrum stops he should be given lots of attention and praise, and some other suitable reward such as a rough and tumble game, listening to a favourite record, holding some favourite object, or a small helping of food or drink.

Most parents who have been faced with daily temper tantrums have in desperation tried to stop the screams by slapping the child. This may have a shock effect the first few times, but if repeated too often the child ceases to take any notice and continues to scream. It is better to reserve this way of reacting for the rare emergency occasion, when something has to be done in a hurry. The method of ignoring the screams and then rewarding the child when he is quiet may take time to work (and requires iron nerves plus deaf ears) but it is the most successful in the end. Both elements are necessary. Ignoring is no use without the eventual reward, and vice versa.

Later on, when the child begins to understand and use words to some extent, he will probably respond to a firm voice and manner when a temper tantrum threatens. He is more likely to be amenable to these 'normal' methods of control if he was treated sensibly and consistently in his earlier years.

Screaming may be due to fear and distress produced by something that is in reality quite harmless. If this goes on for long, the child may lose all control and behave in exactly the same way as in a temper tantrum. It is therefore important to stop the reaction as quickly as possible. When the cause is known, the child can be removed from the fear-provoking situation and comforted. If, as often happens, he refuses all comfort, then the same tactics as for temper tantrums have to be used. The causes of the fear must be tackled, and some suggestions for this will be given further on. It may be impossible to discover the reasons for temper tantrums or for extremes of panic, which in any case are hard to tell apart. In a young child they may be a reaction to the chaos of his life which every now and again becomes unbearable. Careful planning can help to avoid these occasions (see the section on enlarging social experience, below). One special situation which disturbs many young autistic children is waking up from a sleep taken in the daytime. (Many normal people also find this an unpleasant experience.) They often go through a period in which they begin screaming almost as soon as they open their eyes, and cuddling and comforting have no effect. This is commonest around one to two years of age when they are still having a regular daytime nap. Some mothers have found that they can prevent the problem by arranging the timetable so that the child wakes while being pushed along in his pram. The movement seems to be soothing and reassuring. Giving a bottle of fruit juice, singing a nursery rhyme or playing a favourite record immediately on waking may also be effective in preventing the distress.

ii *Destructiveness*

This is a serious problem for many parents. Autistic children cannot play constructively, so they often occupy themselves by examining the simple properties of the things around them. They soon learn that paper (including books and wallpaper) tears, and that many hard things make a noise when hurled to the floor, and an even more satisfying noise when they break. One small boy developed an unerring aim with his toy bricks, and shattered all the light bulbs in his house. At a later stage, the children develop enough to want to fit one object inside another. They often do not comprehend that large into small won't go, so they break and tear to achieve their aim, perhaps having a temper tantrum from frustration at the same time. The products of excretion are easily available, and smearing the walls is added to the rest of the damage. Those autistic children who are too handicapped to be destructive are less trouble, but need even more help than those who do explore the world in these inconvenient ways.

All children need to go through a period of messy play, and some compromise is necessary. Sand, water and mud are less trouble in the garden. If possible, an area especially for the child can be fenced off from the rest. This will also preserve the flowers and vegetables which otherwise tend to suffer the same fate as indoor possessions. In the winter or if there is no garden at all, it is worth considering arranging things so that the child has one room in which to make a mess. A tray of sand and some water can be provided. Large, strong, simple objects that are pleasant to feel and to move around are useful at this stage. A blackboard to scribble on may be used later on.

The rest of the house should be out of bounds except under strict supervision. Night-time may be a special problem. The child's bedroom should be safe for him and easily cleaned. If he tears his wallpaper one night when you are asleep, there is not a lot of point in replacing it until this stage is passed. It is better to use a washable paint which cannot be torn away.

The real solution, in the end, is to help the child to become interested in more constructive activities. This takes time, because the child has to reach the stage of development at which he can be helped. In the meantime, the only thing to do is to supervise the child carefully, and take the same kind of precautions as those necessary with a very active toddler.

A reasonable amount of give and take is necessary. The children must learn that they cannot spoil other people's possessions, but they must also have possessions of their own. It is useful to teach a simple formula to indicate ownership such as 'That belongs to Daddy', 'That belongs to Mummy'. Eventually the child will realise that he must not touch the objects which are labelled in this way. If he can talk he can also be taught an appropriate phrase to indicate the things which belong to him.

iii *Socially embarrassing behaviour*

Young normal children inevitably cause acute embarrassment to their parents in public from time to time, providing many funny stories to be laughed at in retrospect. Autistic children do similar things, but they do them more often, they go on doing them for much longer, and they do them with a total lack of inhibitions.

In the early stages, anticipation is essential, to avoid incidents in which the child knocks down a huge display of tins in a supermarket, or grabs bars of chocolate from the shop counter. The children have no idea of psychological barriers and will wander behind counters and into the back premises of shops quite unconcerned. Some of them run away at any opportunity, pursuing a straight course at considerable speed, heedless of all obstacles. Another adult to accompany the mother on shopping expeditions is a help. If this cannot be arranged, walking reins are useful for the toddler. Many mothers have had to keep their child firmly strapped in the push chair while near any 'danger zones'.

The problem with these restraints is that most autistic children soon learn how to undo them or wriggle out of them. More active teaching is therefore necessary. The child should be watched, and always held firmly as soon as any difficult behaviour begins. At the same time, he should be told 'No' in a firm clear voice. He will begin to realise that 'No' is a strict prohibition and eventually the word will suffice. 'Don't touch' is another phrase which can be taught, by using it whenever you pull your child's hand away from something he must not handle. Autistic children learn these things more slowly than normal children. The period before they have learnt is bound to be difficult and wearing for the parents. They will be tempted to give up and perhaps avoid going out with the child at all, doing the shopping at inconvenient times when they can do it alone. This is a most unsatisfactory solution, because the child loses the opportunity of eventually learning reasonable behaviour.

Fortunately, older autistic children are easier in this respect, but other problems arise with the child who can talk. The children's habit of echoing words and phrases they have heard in the past can lead to unfortunate consequences. Parents have to be especially careful of the things they say in front of their child if they do not want them repeated in an exact copy of their accents and tone of voice. Swear words are particularly easy to learn because the emphasis and intensity usually accompanying them catch the attention of even a withdrawn child. Naive remarks about other people, made in a loud voice, have to be discouraged firmly. Children who can talk enough to make such remarks usually have fairly good comprehension of simple ideas. They will eventually learn that they must never talk about people's appearances, clothes or manners, if they are told many times over, using the same simple words each time. They will not understand the reason for the rule, nor will they be able to generalise to other situations, but the more advanced children may begin to realise that thoughtless remarks can make other people unhappy.

The older child's lack of appreciation of social taboos often leads to problems, especially in those children who appear normal upon superficial observation. Removing clothes or passing urine in public may be done in all innocence by an adolescent or young adult. Parents and teachers have to lay down a series of rules in an attempt to forestall or prevent a repetition of such incidents. The trouble is that no one can think of everything that might happen, and life seems too short to teach the correct response in every imaginable situation (let alone the unimaginable ones that seem to crop up as often). One can only do what one can and hope for the best. Once a rule is learnt, an autistic child tends to keep it under all circumstances. This leads to problems too, as with the child who learnt that one must always use the lavatory, and then suffered intense discomfort on a long drive in the countryside because he could not be persuaded to break the rule in this special situation.

It is important to remember to show pleasure and appreciation when an outing has passed without a mishap.

iv *Resistance to change*

This particular problem ranks high on the list of symptoms which cause parents the most worry and despair. If not handled properly, a child's insistence on routine can come to dominate the life of the whole family. The parents of one child were unable to invite any guests for a meal because he always screamed violently if the seating arrangements for dining were changed in any way.

The behaviour is the child's pathetic attempt to introduce order into his chaotic world, and this has to be remembered when working out the best way of managing the problem. It is necessary to arrange the child's life so that it has order and pattern. He needs to know what will happen next so that he feels comfortable and secure. Change should be introduced only after preparation. When he is young, it is reasonable for him to have his own chair and his own cup, saucer and plate and place at the table, and his special toy to take to bed.

However, a firm line needs to be drawn, when the resistance to change reaches the point where it interferes with the life of the rest of the family, and also prevents the child himself from moving forward to more constructive activities. It is possible to deal with the problem by consistently refusing to allow the child to continue with his more inconvenient routines. One small girl insisted on holding a tiny piece of photographic negative in the palm of her hand. Whenever the negative became damp, which inevitably happened sooner or later, she screamed until a new dry piece was provided. This was finally solved by ceasing to provide any more pieces. Prolonged temper tantrums resulted but eventually the whole business was forgotten.

Witmer; writing in 1919, described a more difficult problem. In this case, the little boy, Don, refused to part with a card which he held in his hand. If this were removed, he immediately scratched his face quite badly with his fingernails. Witmer arranged for a nurse to stay with the child, holding his hands away from his face, gently but firmly. The child screamed ferociously, and the nurse remained kind, patient but immovable. She stayed with him for several hours, releasing his hands from time to time, but holding him again if his fingers went to his face. Finally he could be left without the card and without harming himself. A slower, but less disturbing, method would have been to cut a tiny piece off the card each night, while Don slept, until it disappeared.

Another complication arises if the child is able to find his special objects for himself. A boy who liked tin lids (which he bent into special shapes) and a girl who liked detergent packets were adept at finding these in cupboards, workshops, dustbins or other people's houses. In this case the children have to be supervised closely until they realise that this activity is forbidden.

Insistence on special routines can be managed in a similar way, by refusing to fit into the child's rigid scheme. If temper tantrums result these can be coped with in the way suggested previously.

Parents worry a great deal as to the effect of preventing a child from carrying out his routines or depriving him of his collections. They wonder if this will produce some kind of emotional damage. They can be reassured that there is no evidence that this will occur. In fact, most parents who have had the courage to stand firm have found that once the problem has been overcome the child's behaviour and their relationship with him tend to improve. He learns that his parents are strong confident people, and also that giving up a routine does not make the world fall to pieces. He has been helped to take a small step forward and all the family gain from the experience.

A more reasonable objection is that when one routine is given up, another comes along to take its place. This is to some extent true, because the children's handicaps make them liable to this kind of behaviour. However, if one problem is overcome successfully, those that follow are easier to manage. In theory it should be possible to remove each difficulty over objects or routines as it occurs. In practice, most parents find that a compromise works well. Some of these habits comfort the child but have no adverse effect on anyone else, and these can be left alone. For example, no problem arises if a child likes to carry a smooth pebble in his pocket, as long as he does not have a tantrum if he loses it, or holds it in his hand so much that it interferes with other activities. A little girl wanted to take a large dustpan with her wherever she went. She gradually accepted the idea that the dustpan could be 'played with' at home but not in public. When she went out she would put it on a special shelf in her toy cupboard, saying 'All ready for come-back'. This formula reassured her and she would go out happily, minus the dustpan.

Once parents have made up their minds to discourage inconvenient habits, it is helpful to tackle a new one that might be troublesome as soon as it appears. The task is easier in the early stages than it is once the routine is well established. A number of mothers take deliberate steps to vary household routines just a little every day so that the children become used to the idea of a certain amount of change. This may seem to contradict my earlier suggestion that autistic children need order in their lives. As usual, what one is aiming for is a workable compromise between too much rigidity on the one hand and too little structure on the other, and in the end each family has to make its own decision depending upon its special needs.

v *Problems with eating*

At least two different factors may be involved in feeding problems and food fads.

Firstly, some autistic children have trouble with controlling the movements of the muscles involved with chewing. They are difficult to wean because they do not know how to cope with lumpy food. (Children born partially deaf and partially blind reject lumpy food even more often than autistic children.) Food that needs chewing has to be introduced slowly, so that the child can practise without being frightened by lumps that are too big or hard for him to manage. One mother found that she had to teach her autistic son to chew by moving his lower jaw with her hands to give him an idea of the movements required.

Speech therapists have developed a series of exercises, involving blowing bubbles, blowing pieces of cotton wool, and retrieving sweet food placed on the lips outside the mouth by using the tip of the tongue. These are designed for any child who has trouble in co-ordinating his tongue and mouth movements, and can be found in some books written for parents with handicapped children. (For example, in the *Individual Learning Programmes* mentioned in the book list at the end.)

The second major reason for feeding problems arises from the children's resistance to change, and their tendency to cling to special routines. All autistic children are more suspicious of new foods than even young normal children. The best way to manage food fads in a normal child is to provide a good mixed diet, and adopt an attitude of casual indifference to how much is eaten, since a normal child can be trusted not to starve. Minor eating problems in autistic children can be dealt with in the same way. If the child takes in adequate quantities of protein, fat, carbohydrate, vitamins and fluid overall, it does not matter if for example he refuses certain kinds of food, or eats only one meal a day. In this situation, there is no need for a mother to cook special food for the autistic child – perhaps because the rest of the family likes carrots and the autistic child never touches them. He can miss a meal occasionally without coming to any harm, and he is more likely to come round to trying something new if he is hungry and knows he will get nothing else.

A useful technique with a child who has some understanding and use of words is to introduce a new food or drink with reference to something similar which goes down well. A girl of eight refused to consider a cup of drinking chocolate, until she was told it was 'chocolate-coffee'. She tasted it and liked it at once.

If a feeding problem starts in a child who has previously eaten reasonably well the parents should make sure that the child does not have some physical illness such as a fever which has made him lose his appetite. If there is any doubt a doctor's advice should be sought. Once it is clear that there is no physical cause which should be treated, the same principles of management apply to this problem as to other difficulties that arise. The child should not be 'rewarded' for refusing food by having constant anxious attention paid to him at every meal time. He should not be pressed to eat at all times of the day, or given unsuitable foods (such as sweets or cakes) just to make sure he eats something. He should be given food at meal times only, and in rather small quantities so that every mouthful is needed because he is hungry. Uneaten food should be removed without comment, and a good long empty gap left until the next meal.

Sometimes problems with food assume major proportions. A number of autistic children go through phases in which their diet is restricted to, for example, hamburgers, or lettuce and bananas. A very few cases have been reported in which the child will eat nothing at all. It almost seems as if the child does not connect up the feeling of inner emptiness with the idea of eating food. The problem may disappear of its own accord after a few days, but if the child persists in eating a severely limited diet, then medical advice is needed. One doctor who specialises in paediatrics admits children with this problem into hospital. There they are gradually introduced to new foods by mixing them in with the one or two things they will eat, as a camouflage. The children are allowed nothing at all between meals, and the food is removed if they refuse to eat. Their physical health can be closely supervised during this period. All of the children treated came to like the new foods and eventually ate a normal diet. The scheme was most successful if mothers were admitted at the same time, and taught how to manage meal times at home, to avoid a relapse. The programme of care also included playtimes and perceptual training, once the child had begun to accept a more reasonable range of food.

Fortunately, extreme feeding problems are rather rare. Minor ones are more common. They are inconvenient but not likely to result in any harm to the child, and can be managed with common sense and confidence.

Children who eat poorly at home may develop hearty appetites when they begin school, helped by the example of the other children and the sensible attitude of the staff.

vi *Special fears*

Some autistic children are always tense and fearful, and almost all of them develop fears of harmless things at some time or other. It is usually difficult to know the origin of the fears, but sometimes it is possible to trace then back to their beginnings. One little girl had a pair of new shoes which were uncomfortable because they rubbed her heels. From then on she screamed and refused to walk if shoes were put on her feet. A small boy put his finger into a bath of water which was a little too hot, and could not be persuaded to enter the bath for years after that, although he was quite happy to sit in the large kitchen sink.

Normal children have similar experiences which may alarm them when they are small, but they can communicate their fears to their parents and accept verbal reassurance and explanation. Autistic children have no way of asking for help, and uncomfortable events tend to confirm their fears of the world and their dislike of any change.

The behaviour which was first caused by fear may continue as a routine habit long after the fear has gone. In this case it can be dealt with in the same way as other routines. Before this stage is reached the problem is more difficult to solve because the child's terror is so obvious, and parents feel acute distress if they try to force the child into situations in which he is fearful.

Sometimes it is possible to change the child's behaviour by gradual exposure to the frightening situation. For example, the little girl who would not wear shoes was helped in the following way. At the time she loved to eat boiled eggs. When she had her egg for tea, a pair of slippers in her favourite colour was placed beside her, while she was eating, and taken away before she had finished. Without the egg the slippers produced screams, but with the egg they were accepted calmly. The time with the slippers was lengthened, and then the stage was reached when they could be put on her feet while she was eating. The time with slippers on was again lengthened until she cheerfully wore them all through tea. After this, her outdoor shoes were tried, and these produced no fearful reaction. She wore them without any fuss, and from then on they were put on in the morning in the usual way. The fear never recurred, and buying new shoes is now looked forward to as a pleasant occasion.

It is not always possible to carry out this kind of plan. Chocolate sweets were tried for the boy who was afraid of the bath tub, but the fear was too strong to be soothed by the sweets. It is interesting that this problem was eventually overcome in a different way. A new *au-pair* girl who was good with children popped him into a bath during the daytime on the first day of her stay with the family, unaware of his fear. His astonished mother heard happy giggles and splashes and found her child enjoying his first bath in years as if he had one every day. The same *au-pair* girl, encouraged by her success, persuaded the same child to use the adult lavatory, of which he had previously been afraid. In this case, it seems that the child was helped by the different expectations of the *au-pair* girl. She was not anticipating fear whereas his parents had grown accustomed to it. They also learnt from the experience, and were much more confident (and successful) in dealing with other similar problems which occurred after this incident. Hair-washing, and hair and nail-cutting is disliked by all young children but may cause intense fear and furious resistance in an autistic child. Since these things have to be done, parents must persist as calmly as they can, and never give up once they have started, even if one person has to hold the child while the other washes or trims. Eventually the problem eases and passes away, especially if the child becomes interested in his appearance. Visits to a hairdresser who is good with children should be started as early as possible so that this becomes an accepted routine.

It usually happens that once the child is persuaded to face the things that frighten him his fears dissolve away. An autistic girl refused to do more than stand in the water at the seaside and screamed if anyone tried to hold her with her feet off the bottom. One day she suddenly found that she was able to float with her special arm bands and swimming ring, and from that moment she was utterly without fear of the sea (although this had its inconvenient side too).

Some families have dealt with their child's fear of dogs by buying a puppy. This usually works well although it is wise to choose a dog from a reputable breeder and of a type that is likely to be placid and good with children when it grows up. It is also sensible to prepare the child by showing him pictures of dogs, and toy models of dogs in advance.

It should be remembered that autistic children can develop certain fears because of their sensitivity to loud noises and bright lights. This may lie behind fears of, for example, aeroplanes, trains, motor bikes, barking dogs and photographers' flash lights. They seem to find these stimuli quite painful, and are not making a fuss about nothing. Calm reassurance and distraction of the child's attention may help. Fortunately the sensitivity becomes less troublesome as time goes on. Sympathy for the child should not prevent one from being fairly firm about riding in trains or aeroplanes if these journeys are necessary. Once inside, most of the children find the noise level tolerable, and in any case they nearly all enjoy the movement, so that fear gives place to pleasure.

The children tend to be confused if they wake in the night. This is also true of normal children and adults if they wake suddenly from a deep sleep, but the problem seems more severe and longer lasting in autistic children. They may appear particularly fearful and distressed in these circumstances, and are hard to comfort because they resist being touched or cuddled. They may be soothed by a reassuring manner, a calm and gentle tone of voice, and perhaps hearing a favourite song or nursery rhyme.

Each fear has to be considered, and a decision made whether to deal with it by slowly increasing exposure linked with something that is enjoyed, or by showing the child at once that there is nothing to be frightened of, or else by allowing the child to avoid the situation until he can be helped to overcome it at a later stage.

The key to the problem is confidence. If the parents feel confident in what they are doing, then the child will respond and the difficulties will be resolved. Once this has happened, of course, it is easier to have confidence in one's ability to solve the next problem. It is taking the first step which is so hard. Experienced teachers have a natural advantage over parents in these matters, because they have been through similar situations many times before, and no longer feel worried and unsure of themselves. It often happens, therefore, that a seemingly insoluble problem dissolves away when the child starts to attend school.

vii *Lack of fear of real dangers*

This is the opposite side of the picture to the children's special fears, but can be equally worrying. Many parents remember how their child walked into the water, fully clothed, on his first visit to the seaside. The children who like climbing tend to have at least one heart-stopping feat to their credit, such as walking along a narrow ledge on the roof or hanging out of the window practically by their toes. They are usually so sure-footed that no harm results, but there have been a few instances in which children have been injured or even killed because they were oblivious of real danger.

Parents have to be aware of this. They can teach the rules for crossing the road, avoiding fires, electricity and gas, and warn the children of other common dangers, but even the brightest autistic child will learn these by rote, and may not apply them to a new situation. It may be necessary to put bars on a young child's window, and to keep various doors in the house locked. The keys should be kept in a place which cannot be reached by a child because the children may have no difficulty in learning how to undo locks. All possible sources of danger both inside and outside the house have to be considered and proper precautions organised. As with every other problem, the worst time is between two and five years of age. The children do tend to become more aware of danger as they grow older – at least they are more willing to obey the rules.

viii *Odd movements and grimaces*

The children's tendency to show odd movements is a problem for two main reasons. Firstly they look peculiar and draw undesirable attention in public. Secondly, the children seem to derive some satisfaction or stimulation from their movements and grimaces, and may keep them up for hours, rather than engage in any constructive activity.

If an adult works with a child and involves him in some occupation, the odd movements hardly occur at all. They are at their worst when the child has nothing to do. Therefore one of the most useful ways of dealing with this behaviour is to occupy the child as fully as possible. It is not desirable to try to stop all the odd movements completely since this seems to make the children tense, but they need to be limited to certain times and places.

The movements have to be discouraged when out shopping, on outings or anywhere in public. Gently holding the child's hands when he twists and turns them gradually gives him the idea that this behaviour is not acceptable. The action can be linked with a word or phrase so that eventually this alone will remind him.

ix *Self-injury*

This is yet another problem that autistic children share with children who are born both deaf and blind. Like the odd movements it occurs more often if the children are unoccupied. It is most obvious in children who live in large understaffed institutions, and who have to be left to their own devices for most of the time. The major part of the solution is therefore the organising of the child's day to give him plenty to do.

Psychologists who are specially interested in methods of behaviour modification describe how children in institutions often receive attention from the staff only when they begin to harm themselves. The staff may run to comfort them, or to scold them, when this happens, but otherwise the children may be ignored. It is easy to see how this will make the self-injury occur more often than ever, although it started originally because the child was bored and unoccupied. Some workers have tried to stop serious self-injury in children by punishing this behaviour, and giving the child praise and attention only when he is not biting, scratching or head-banging. These methods have been used because the self-injury had gone on so long and had assumed such alarming proportions. The individual attention and stimulation of family life is the best way of preventing this distressing behaviour.

Even when they are living at home the children do sometimes bite, or hurt themselves in other ways. This may happen because of some minor frustration, or when the child becomes upset and confused through his inability to understand. (This is bound to happen from time to time even in the best possible environment.) The children often bite the backs of their wrists and hands, and look very tense and angry when they do this. The best way to deal with this situation is to sort out the confusion (perhaps a misunderstanding of verbal instructions) or to take some action concerning the reason for the frustration, depending on its cause.

Self-injury in a well-cared-for child may also occur during a temporary period of unhappiness. The parents of one little girl of eight years old were away from home for a week, leaving her with someone whom she knew and liked. While they were away she tended to pick at sore places and even prick her fingers with an open safety pin. She needed a lot of extra care and comforting during this time, especially since she could not use words to express her feelings nor understand enough to know when her parents were due to return. It may require much patience and detailed knowledge of the child to discover the source of the unhappiness unless it is as obvious as in the case I described. The sudden occurrence of this symptom in an autistic child should be a signal for the parents to look for a cause.

x *The very withdrawn child*

So far I have described the difficult behaviour of autistic children who are active and react to their handicaps with a kind of angry determination. There are other children who respond in a different way. They are quiet and withdrawn, tending to isolate themselves from the world, rather than hitting their heads against it in rage and frustration. They may be unchildlike in their neatness and cleanliness, because they never explore their environment, and have no interest in mud, sand or water. In contrast to the active autistic child who climbs to the top shelf of the cupboard to reach forbidden objects and undoes locks in a way that Houdini would have envied, the passive children may do nothing for themselves. They give the impression that their hands lack the strength even to lift a spoon to their mouths, or to handle a toy which is placed in front of them.

This kind of child gives less practical trouble than those who are full of energy, but they tend to be far more aloof, and cause their parents deep sadness and anxiety for this reason. In some ways, also, it is easier for a mother to feel she has something positive to do when she has to cope with an active 'naughty' child. The self-contained passive child makes most parents feel lost, helpless and worst of all, unnecessary and unwanted.

The task of the parents here is to lead the child into the world by showing him that it is not a fearful place, and that efforts produce enjoyable consequences. This involves encouraging the child, rather than restraining his behaviour, and the suggestions under the headings of 'Teaching basic skills' and 'Enlarging social experience' may be of help. The book *The Siege*, written by Clara Claiborne Park, who is a parent of a child of this kind, gives an excellent and moving description of the way in which she helped her autistic daughter, together with much detailed advice which other parents can follow.

TEACHING BASIC SKILLS

This section is not intended to persuade parents to take on the role of teachers. Some parents have had to shoulder the whole burden of the education of their autistic child by themselves, because there was no alternative, and they have sometimes succeeded remarkably well. However, it is only the rare person with no other commitments, plus a genuine flair for teaching, who can take on the task. The roles of teacher and parent are hard to combine, and the ideal solution is for the handicapped child to live at home and to attend a special school. He then gets the best of both worlds.

Nevertheless, parents teach their normal children the simple skills of everyday living, and social relationships, and they need to know how to teach their autistic children the same things. Most people manage to bring up a normal child in the light of the ideas on child-rearing which are commonly held in their particular culture. These ideas are modified by experience but are useful as a rough and ready guide. Autistic children are a different problem altogether. It seems to the bewildered parents that none of the ordinary rules and expectations apply at all. They have rather the same emotions as a sparrow faced with a cuckoo in her nest – but, like the sparrow, they have little time for philosophical speculations and have to get on with the job as best they can.

In fact the rules which psychologists have found to govern the process of learning do apply to autistic children, but as usual the application in practice has to be modified to fit in with the problems of a child who cannot talk and cannot understand language.

The first of these rules I have already mentioned in relation to managing difficult behaviour, but it is worth repeating. Children (and adults as well) are likely to learn behaviour which is 'rewarded' (meaning that the behaviour has consequences which are enjoyable for the person concerned) and are likely to refrain from behaviour which has unpleasant results.

The second rule is that new skills are learned more easily if they are broken down into very tiny simple steps, instead of being presented all at once. This is reflected in the old saying, 'You must learn to walk before you can run.' Autistic children are especially liable to be upset by failure, and making sure that the child can succeed with each small stage is a good way of avoiding this problem.

Thirdly, a child can be encouraged to try a new skill by prompting him, fairly obviously at first, then less and less as time goes on.

The fourth rule is that it is helpful to link new learning with skills which are already familiar and which give pleasure. This is particularly appropriate for autistic children whose interest is hard to rouse. A special example of this rule is the use of a well learned skill as an aid in acquiring a new idea. A child may be able to understand the meaning of 'large' and 'small' but not be able to name colours. The first step is to make sure that he is not colour blind by finding out if he can sort a mixture of different coloured buttons into single colour piles. If this can be done, the next step is to select two colours, and then make a single large square of one colour (for example red), and a series of squares of the other colour (for example green) ranging from very small up to the size of the one large red square. Then the child is shown the large red square and the smallest green square. He is told the names of the colours and taught (by rewarding if necessary) to name, or point to, red or green when told. He will learn this because he can already name 'large' and 'small' and he will take his cue from the size of the squares, ignoring the colour. The series of green squares is then shown to the child, in ascending order of size, one after the other. Each time he has to name or point to red and green. Somewhere along the line, as the squares become more and more alike in size, he will realise that it is the colour he is supposed to name and not the size. The penny may drop suddenly and the child will show a flash of understanding and intense pleasure. It is usually unnecessary to teach all colour names in this way once the first two are learnt. The rest come by pointing them out and naming them. This technique, well known to psychologists, can be adapted for learning other skills.

It is important, when considering how to teach an autistic child a new skill, to have detailed knowledge of his handicaps. This point is ignored by some of the psychologists working in the field, although others are keenly aware of its relevance. To take one example, a child may be unable to distinguish and name the letters of the alphabet correctly. One possible reason is that he has a general problem of comprehension which prevents him from understanding which aspects of a particular letter determine its name. For example, a normal child can be told that *b* is a complete circle attached to an up-stroke on the left, but *c* has no up-stroke, and is an incomplete circle. An autistic child will not understand this explanation and may name the letters according to their size alone, even though he can see the other differences. A second possible reason for the inability to distinguish two letters is that he cannot see that they are different because of his special handicaps. This is likely to occur in the case of the letters *b* and *d*, which are mirror images of each other, if the child has difficulty in distinguishing left from right.

In the first case, the method of teaching colour names described above can be successfully adapted to teaching the names of letters. In the second case, the method will be unsuccessful, and the moment of understanding as the letter sizes approach each other will not occur. Instead the child may become anxious and distressed. The problem is shown clearly when a child can learn to distinguish *a* and *c*, but not *b* and *d*. In this case it is clear that the difficulty is not due to lack of co-operation but to a problem of perception. For each particular child and for each particular learning problem, it is necessary to determine the reason for the difficulty, and then to plan one's teaching methods on the basis of this knowledge. Unfortunately, there are as yet few teachers who are experienced in the problems of autistic children, and no specialised training is available.

Autistic children tend to go through phases in which they make little or no progress, and then, suddenly, they acquire a new skill, or take a step forward in language and social development. Sometimes they appear to learn something without preliminary practice, as with the boy of nine who tied his own shoelaces one day, after his mother had tied them for him every morning up to that time. Occasionally a child will perform a new skill once only and then revert to his previous behaviour, and it may be many years before he tries again. It is realistic to expect a slow rate of progress, on a different time-scale from that of a normal child. On the other hand, it is some comfort to know that, in most autistic children, improvement (slow but perceptible) continues throughout childhood, adolescence and adult life. There is no justification for the idea that there is a definite age limit beyond which no further change can be expected.

i *General co-operation*

Life becomes easier and happier if you can teach your child to come when you call his name, to sit down with you for a while, and to accept and enjoy the physical contact that is necessary for non-verbal learning.

Parents tend to use all kinds of pet names for their children, including versions of their given names. This is fun to do, and is a demonstration of family love and solidarity, but while an autistic child is learning to know his name it is probably best to use one only that is agreed by everyone. Once he does respond to this name, there is no problem about learning the other versions.

To begin with, the child's name should always be used in connection with situations which are pleasant for him. For example, if he is the kind of child who enjoys his meals, you should call his name as you prepare to give him his food. If he can see the plate coming, and is looking forward to eating his dinner, the sound of his name will begin to have happy associations. The name should be used in other situations as well, to make sure that he does not learn that 'Johnny' means 'dinner' and nothing else. When you give him a drink, a biscuit, a sweet, or call him to get ready for a walk (showing him what is intended by holding his coat ready to put on) or while you prepare for an enjoyable activity, you can use his name to gain his attention. At first you will probably have to hold his hand and lead him towards the food, or whatever it is you are arranging, saying his name at the same time. This kind of teaching is easier to manage if two adults work together, one leading the child and the other calling his name and showing him his coat, food, drink of whatever is appropriate. In time, the name alone will be sufficient. You can then use a simple phrase like 'Johnny – dinner' or 'Johnny – walk', 'Johnny – orange juice' so that he can learn that his name is to make him look round or come, and the second word tells him what will happen.

In the early stages do not use his name when you are angry, because this could have the reverse effect of your special teaching. It is also sensible not to use his name a great deal in situations where you do not want him to respond. You should, for instance, avoid discussing him in his presence, because this allows him to fall back into the habit of hearing his name spoken but ignoring it.

I have already mentioned the necessity of teaching the meaning of 'No' and 'Don't touch' when discussing socially embarrassing behaviour. These are prohibitions, and have to be taught by combining the words with physically preventing the child from carrying out the forbidden act. Once you have stopped him, and removed the temptation, you must not show anger or continue using the sharp tone that went with the word 'No'. He has done what you wanted (even if it was because you gave him no choice), therefore he should enjoy your love and approval. There is little point in learning to do what mother says if she continues to be cross and irritable afterwards. Later on when he can talk and when he can remember, then it may be useful to disapprove of bad behaviour some time after it has occurred (if for instance, you find out about it too late to prevent it), but this can only be done when the child has reached the appropriate stage of development

Some autistic children struggle against certain kinds of physical contact. They usually enjoy tickling and being swung round and other fairly vigorous play. This can be used to lead on to more gentle touching and cuddling. The usual pattern can be followed of associating contact with other enjoyable experiences such as the mid-morning orange-juice drink, a meal, listening to a record, or singing a nursery rhyme. It may be necessary to start with a few seconds of contact only and then gradually to increase the time. The child has to learn to accept and enjoy your touch so that you can guide him while he is learning various useful skills.

Sitting quietly on a chair has to be learnt in small stages in the same way. An autistic child can learn that he will not have his food unless he sits quietly at the meal table. Some families find every mealtime a nightmare because their handicapped child insists on eating his food in snatches while running round the room. There is not much point in keeping a young child sitting at table waiting for everyone else to finish but he should stay at least until he has finished his own meal. Later on, he has to learn to wait for others if he is to have the pleasure of eating in restaurants with the rest of the family, but this can be taught gradually.

Sitting at a table in order to play with puzzles or to draw comes as part of the process of gaining interest in the occupation. Once these activities are enjoyed by the child it is not difficult to show him that he can only have the equipment as long as he is willing to sit and play with it, and that when he becomes restless it will be put away.

I have several times mentioned using food and meal-times as an aid to learning. This idea arouses strong opposition in some people, because they feel that this is 'training' rather than teaching, and that using basic needs as motives is not appropriate for children. The answer is that with a very young severely handicapped child who cannot understand any of the usual ways of teaching, one has to use whatever is at hand to help the child 'catch on' to what is wanted. Food is the easiest and surest thing to start with (as long as the child enjoys eating and does not have a food problem), but there are plenty of other rewards that can be used later. Going out for a walk, listening to records, hearing nursery songs, tickling and cuddling, whispering into the child's ear, playing with water, riding in a car, giving a pick-a-back ride can all be used depending on the child's special likes and dislikes. Parents soon find that even if they have to start with food, they can go on to other kinds of rewards, and eventually their approval will be sufficient, although it may not be enough when starting a new activity. Anyone with practical experience of young autistic children would agree that it is better for a child to start helping him as soon as possible, rather than to refuse to use food as a reward because of theoretical objections.

A more practical problem is that the foods most liked by children tend to be sweets and biscuits. If these are used between meals they spoil the appetite for more nutritious food, may lead to overweight, and furthermore, they are bad for the teeth. If the child likes little pieces of apple or other fruit, these problems are less serious. Conventional mealtimes can be used for teaching. If there is no choice but to use sweets, then tiny pieces of a variety that does not have to be chewed (plus good general dental care) are the best compromise. Other ways of motivating the child should be used as soon as possible.

ii *Resistance to learning and negativism*

Autistic children, when they are young, appear to be resistant to learning new skills. Sometimes they seem to refuse to do anything that is required of them. When a skill is learnt, a child may repeat it again and again until its performance seems meaningless, and he may resist any attempt to move on to another task. Careful observation of the situations in which the children respond with stubborn resistance to, or a withdrawal from, teaching, will begin to give some idea of the reasons for this behaviour.

Some children show more resistance than others. Usually, the more a child is able to talk and to comprehend language, the less negative behaviour he shows. Even the most stubborn child is more willing to work at some tasks than at others. The important factor seems to be how much the child understands what you want him to do. If he cannot guess from what you are saying, and has trouble imitating the things he sees you doing, it is not particularly surprising that he does the wrong thing, or does nothing at all. Depending on the personality of the child concerned, continued attempts to make him perform might lead to a temper tantrum, severe anxiety, or to withdrawal.

Although the basic problem underlying a negative attitude is a genuine lack of understanding, there is no doubt that secondary difficulties arise. Confusion is a most unpleasant emotion, and repeated failure is depressing. The children come to associate every teaching situation with these unhappy feelings, and start to react against learning almost as soon as a task is presented. In this they are no different from an otherwise normal child who has a specific difficulty with reading, and who develops emotional disturbances as a consequence of his primary handicap. Many of the children become upset if their mistakes are corrected when they have begun to learn a new skill. They may scream, bite the backs of their hands, and appear to be anxious and distressed. This in turn upsets the teacher, and an inexperienced person may be frightened to continue. The problem can be minimised by making sure that the explanations are simple. If a child makes a mistake, the steps in learning may have to be made even smaller. It helps to remain calm and confident and reassuring. If you feel the child can succeed, you must be firm, and show that he has to try, but without losing your temper. Your confidence will communicate itself to the child.

Another factor complicating the children's learning problems may have a physical cause. Some parents notice that their autistic children seem to have good days and bad days. Sometimes they are more alert, more interested in the world, and more willing to learn. At other times, perhaps even the next day, they are withdrawn, irritable, and refuse to co-operate. These swings are most marked in the early years. Occasionally parents say that they notice that their child's appearance is subtly different on his bad days, his face being puffy and his eyes tired – although this may follow the crying and temper tantrums rather than preceding them. If a child sometimes co-operates well and sometimes refuses to do anything, he may not be 'trying to be awkward' – his handicaps may be harder to overcome on some days than on others, for reasons beyond his control. In any case, if someone is trying to perform at the upper limits of his skill his performance will be far more variable than it would be if he were working well within his resources. The ups and downs shown by world-class sportsmen in important matches are an example of an extreme situation, but an autistic child has to work just as hard to cope with everyday life.

Careful attention to correct methods of teaching helps to overcome the problems caused by lack of understanding. The child can be given tasks prepared in such a way that he has a chance of succeeding and when he does succeed he should be shown approval in ways that he can understand. Under these conditions so-called 'negativism' becomes much less troublesome, as long as training is not pushed beyond the child's capabilities.

There is no point in trying to teach an autistic child a new skill before the age at which one would expect success with a normal child. In fact, since most autistic children are retarded in development, teaching is more likely to succeed if it is started rather later than it would be with normal children. If, after trying to teach a child, it becomes obvious that his handicaps prevent him from learning some particular task, it should be left for a while and then tried again. It requires considerable insight and judgment to decide at any particular stage if increased pressure will help a child to succeed, or if it will intensify his confusion and anxiety. There is no easy answer to this problem and parents and teachers have to decide in the light of their knowledge of and feeling for the child, and their past experience. Some mistakes are inevitable but fortunately their effects are by no means irrevocable.

I shall now mention a few of the areas in which parents can help their children at home.

iii *Toilet training*

Some autistic children are toilet-trained at the same time as the average normal child. Others remain incontinent for several years. The same training methods can be used as with normal children, but they require patience and persistence. The best thing is not to make any fuss about the child's mistakes, but to put him on his pot or on the lavatory regularly at the times when he is most likely to use them. These are on waking after a dry night or daytime sleep, after meals and after drinks given between meals. Each child has to be observed carefully so that the time between eating or drinking, and emptying bowels or bladder can be worked out fairly accurately. He should remain on his pot or on the lavatory for a few minutes. If successful he should be given lots of praise and attention, or some other reward which he likes. If nothing happens, no comment should be made.

Some children seem to dislike or even fear the pot or toilet seat. It is worth while finding out if they feel insecure. Small pot-chairs can be bought which are stable and comfortable. An adult-size lavatory may be too high off the ground for a small child, so something to place his feet on will help. A very cold toilet seat will be enough to worry some children.

Even with patience and persistence, it may be a long time before an autistic child can go without nappies. People who write on child care advise parents that they should change a wet or soiled nappy as soon as possible, so that the child does not become used to being wet, and therefore unconcerned about the discomfort.

iv *Self-care*

This includes dressing, using knife, fork and spoon, washing, brushing and combing hair, cleaning teeth and all the other necessities of daily living. Normal children, encouraged by their parents, try to imitate these activities which they see performed by other members of the family. When they are strong enough and well co-ordinated enough they begin to co-operate in the care given by their mothers, and soon want to take over these functions for themselves. They want to try feeding themselves and dressing themselves even if they make a mess in the process. Autistic children, on the other hand, may go through a phase, around one or two years of age, of actively resisting attempts to wash and dress them. Every item of daily care may precipitate a tantrum at this stage. Later on they tend to accept all these attentions passively, like little dolls rather than children.

Teaching them to care for themselves involves a method which can be applied in many different situations. The children cannot learn by being *told* how, nor by being *shown* how, but they can learn by *feeling* how to do things. If a child's limbs and fingers are held and moved through the pattern of movements necessary for a particular skill he will eventually realise what is required of him. If you want him to do up his buttons, you should choose a garment with large buttons and easy buttonholes on the front, within reach of his fingers. You stand behind him and hold his hands firmly but not too tightly so that you can put them through the movements necessary for fastening the buttons. You can encourage him while you do this if he likes to hear you speak, but if he is the kind of child who becomes worried and upset by talking while he is involved in a new task, it is best to keep silent. You can hug and praise him when the buttons are done up. One button is probably enough to start with.

At first his fingers will feel limp, and you will find that you are doing all the work. This may last for weeks, but eventually you will begin to feel some tension in his hands. Little by little he will follow your movements until in the end he is doing the job himself. He will probably continue to need the touch of your hand on his arm to encourage him for some time, but in the end you can remove even this support, and doing up his own buttons will become second nature to him.

Most self-care skills can be taught by breaking them into

simple steps. It is often best to teach the last step first and work backwards so the child is always the one to finish the job. Dressing is rather a special problem because it involves putting things on the right way out and the right way round. If you consider all the operations involved in putting on a pullover with the seams inside and the V-neck in front, you can see that it is a most complicated activity. Autistic children who are confused about up-down, back-front and right-left will learn to put their clothes on, but will need extra help for a long time if the result is to be acceptable. To start with, it will be necessary to place the clothes in front of the child so that they will end up in the correct position, and give a guiding hand when necessary. Later on, helpful labels which should go inside and at the back can be pointed out to the child, but success requires years of practice.

Brushing and combing hair involves using a mirror for a presentable result. Problems of right-left orientation therefore complicate this skill also, and complete success depends on practice plus increasing maturity.

The children should be encouraged to feed themselves even if they are messy eaters. They may have to use a spoon and fork for a long time, but eventually they should be able to graduate to a knife and fork. Some of them find problems in co-ordinating a knife and fork for cutting food (as in the English method of eating) and may prefer the American style of eating pre-cut food with a fork alone.

One special problem is that autistic children do not have much conception of a finished result. They do not put the final touches to dressing, such as tucking shirt inside trousers, or pulling up the socks neatly. Hair tends to be brushed the requisite number of times without regard to the actual style in which it is supposed to be worn, and face and hands may be washed with vigour, but without removing streaks of dirt on areas left untouched by the operation. They are often unaware of which clothes are suitable for the prevailing weather, and will put on thick underclothes in the summer, or light cotton dresses in the winter. Supervision and tactful assistance (without nagging) have to be available, and are usually necessary even for adolescents and adults.

An interest in clothes and general appearance is a good thing to encourage. It is worth while taking extra trouble to dress a girl, or a boy for that matter, so that he or she looks as neat and attractive as possible. This is a help towards being accepted socially, and also gives plenty of opportunity for people to make nice remarks to the child. As they grow older the children begin to realise that all this is pleasant and they learn to be concerned about their clothes and enjoy expeditions to buy new ones. This is a happy contrast to the early years in which many autistic children bitterly resent any attempt to try on garments in shops.

v *Helping in the home*

Handicapped children are dependent for so long and need so much special care that they tend to become completely passive members of their families. It is better for them if they have some positive role to play, however limited this may be. Autistic children, once they have become reasonably co-operative and willing to learn, can be taught many simple tasks. Laying the table with cutlery is a good one to begin with, since there is nothing to break if dropped. It has the special advantage that it involves remembering and naming each person in the family who has a place at table. Each one has the same implements, and this gives the opportunity of learning to use and understand the words 'knife', 'fork' and 'spoon'. Many children will have difficulty in knowing on which side to place the knives and forks, but this is all good practice in learning left from right. The process is begun by putting things in the child's hands, taking him to the table and guiding his hand to lay the places. All the family should show their appreciation of his help.

Clearing the table, putting out the milk bottles, carrying a small shopping bag, pushing a trolley in a supermarket, wheeling a small wheelbarrow in the garden can all be taught if you have enough patience. Jobs which are quick to perform and finish are best to start with. It is more difficult to persuade the children to persist at an endless task like clearing leaves from the garden lawn. They cannot understand the purpose and soon wander away. When they are older they may become better at these rather boring occupations.

If a task involves a sequence of operations, young autistic children often forget the steps involved. One little girl of seven was helping in the garden by taking a basket full of weeds to the compost heap. She set off down the long garden path, then after a few yards she stopped and looked puzzled. Her father repeated the instructions, her face cleared and she set off again, only to stop once more. She finally reached the destination and disposed of the weeds, but had to have the separate instructions repeated four times altogether. After a while she had the whole task clear in her mind and could carry it out unaided. The children need much attention to prevent them from losing interest because they cannot carry in their minds all the steps involved in a job.

vi *Physical activities*

Since autistic children have little capacity for creative play, it is especially useful to encourage physical activities which are enjoyable without the need for imagination.

Swings and slides and rocking horses are usually popular. The more anxious autistic children may refuse to try them, but it is worth while persevering to overcome the fear because of the pleasure to be found in these activities. If the child is taken to the local park he must be watched carefully at first, because he may run straight into a swing being used by another child without being aware of the danger. He will also have to learn to take his turn. This is a valuable lesson but there may be many temper tantrums and painful scenes while it is being learnt. Once a child realises that this kind of behaviour means a swift exit from the playground, he will begin to accept the waiting with better grace.

Riding a tricycle can be taught with the help of two adults. One should guide the child's feet round the pedals and the other should hold his hands on the handlebars. When he experiences the necessary movements he will begin to pedal for himself. Riding a two-wheeled cycle is much more difficult since it involves balance as well as muscular effort. Some autistic children learn this with surprising ease but some never succeed. It sometimes happens that a child is given a bicycle at seven or eight years of age, but he does not learn to ride and soon loses interest. The bicycle is put away and forgotten until, several years later, the child's parents are amazed to see him pedalling it along the garden path as if he had been able to ride all his life.

ENLARGING SOCIAL EXPERIENCE

Some people have questioned whether it is desirable to modify the behaviour of autistic children and to teach them things the purpose of which they cannot understand. These people have, on the whole, worked on the theory that if the children are in a loving environment they will in time become normal. It is sad that experience has shown that this does not happen. The children who make most progress are those who are given an opportunity to learn in an ordered, structured environment.

One of the reasons for this is that the basic learning of reasonable behaviour and the simple skills of living opens the way to a wider range of social experience which is denied to the child who is too difficult to be taken out.

i *Exploring the world*

The children can make the most of social experience when they reach the stage at which the world makes some sense to them – when they can predict at least a few simple consequences of the things that happen. Parents and teachers have to help autistic children build up a picture of the world brick by brick. The process is started by encouraging the children to explore the world to the best of their ability. Many of them show their immaturity in the way they examine themselves, other people and objects. At the age of four or five years an autistic child may still regard his own hand emerging from a sleeve as if he had not seen it before. He may bend down to look at things backwards through his legs, or try the effect of pulling the corners of his eyelids, and filling his eyes with tears, apparently to see whether the world appears different that way. This is strongly reminiscent of the description given by the psychologist Piaget of the normal very young child who regarded her own feet from different viewpoints, at the time when she was still too immature to realise that objects remain the same even though their appearance changes depending on the angle from which they are seen. Games and songs involving touching and tickling ('This little piggy', 'Round and round the garden') are useful because they teach the child about his own body as well as making him laugh.

There are surprising gaps in the world of an autistic child. He may not realise that his own house is a separate entity from the other houses in the row. It is a good idea to point out to him the windows and the door, and the boundaries which separate the house and garden from the others next door. Drawing and naming afterwards is also useful.

When the child is beginning to take some interest in the world, you can help by making sure that he knows what is going on and why things happen. For example, if the family car has to be repaired, you can tell him in simple words that the car has gone away, and the man in the garage will mend it. If there are many visible signs, such as a dented bumper, he can look at that before and after the repair. If he goes to the garage with you he can say 'Bye bye, car, see you another day' or whatever phrase you know he will understand.

Some children are interested in road works and building operations. If these are going on in the neighbourhood, they can be included in the daily walk so that progress can be seen and commented upon. It is always safest to assume that an autistic child does not understand the reason for any event in his environment, unless you can explain it to him in as simple a way as possible, and continue to repeat the explanation at every opportunity.

ii *Language and communication*

Success in teaching an autistic child to communicate depends to a great extent on his in-built potential, which in turn depends upon the severity of his handicaps. Given this inherent limitation, however, a great deal can be done to help a child to use his given potential to the full.

Psychologists who are interested in the processes of learning have given much attention to the problem of teaching autistic children to speak and to use language. They have developed methods of building speech from the simplest sounds that the child can make, by rewarding each tiny step forward. The work done by these psychologists on managing behaviour problems, discussed earlier, has been successful. There is more doubt about the eventual effect of teaching language in the same way. Many children who were previously mute do learn to say words and even phrases, but so far no strong evidence has been produced to show that their ability to use language in a mature and flexible fashion improves at the same time. It is to be hoped that future work will clarify this whole problem.

As far as parents are concerned, unless they have special training, they cannot put these detailed techniques into practice at home. They can, however, learn one or two useful lessons from the psychologists. A child is more likely to attempt to produce words if his parents do not supply all his needs before he has tried to say anything. Parents easily get into this habit to avoid temper tantrums, but once they become confident in dealing with this behaviour, they can begin to use everyday situations to help the child to make some effort to speak. The first steps in achieving understanding and use of words, and the basis of good pronunciation, are similar for all kinds of children with severe language problems. They are described clearly in the book by Jeffree and McConkey (see book list). In the rest of this section I shall concentrate on the difficulties which are special to autistic children.

Almost everyone tends to assume that autistic children understand more than they really do. To begin with they echo long phrases that sometimes, by coincidence, make sense. Later on they begin to pick up some simple clues from people's gestures. When they do learn to speak they sometimes acquire a large vocabulary which gives the impression that they understand a lot. If you listen to the way they make sentences and the ideas they express, it is clear that, despite the large number of words they know, their comprehension is limited. It is therefore best to use simple language when talking to an autistic child.

With a child who is only just beginning to understand, you should limit your speech to short phrases that you are sure he will understand. This is difficult to do. The normal thing is for mothers to chatter away to their children, simplifying a bit but using many extra words beyond those necessary to convey meaning. This is appropriate for a normal child because it helps him to learn new words and new grammatical structures. An autistic child on the other hand is confused by all the extra words. He is more likely to learn to come in response to 'Johnny – dinner' than to 'Come along, Johnny darling, you will have to hurry up because your dinner is getting cold'.

As time goes on the phrases can include more words. The aim is to make sure that the child understands, but to keep a tiny way ahead of him so that he can learn new words and sentences at a speed which is reasonable for him. Careful speech, limited in quantity, does not come naturally to adults. It has to be practised with conscious effort. The children are more likely to attend to words which are emphasised, so it helps to stress the important words in each sentence. Some autistic children can understand words that are sung to a tune more easily than those which are spoken. Singing words is an excellent way of increasing the child's interest in speech and willingness to try for himself.

The first words learnt are usually the names of things that the child uses. Autistic children find it especially hard to realise that many nouns refer to more than one object. They may call the dining-room chair a chair, but not realise that the same word applies to chairs of a different shape or size. Another kind of mistake occurs when they do generalise but select the wrong characteristic as a basis for generalisation. One girl learnt to name a circle, but then used the label for many other things (such as lamp-shades, steering wheels and so on) which were circular in one dimension, and whose real names she did not know. Parents can help by naming things for the child, and giving him time to repeat the words. You can never assume that a child can name even the commonest objects unless you have specifically taught him. Normal children learn from casual conversation which they hear all day and every day, but autistic children seem unable to do this. On the rare occasions when they do pick things up casually they are liable to get them wrong. An autistic boy heard his father say 'It's about time I washed the car' and immediately rushed to get his coat in preparation for a ride in the car. The children may invent some delightful names for things when in doubt. 'Candlestick' for mushroom, 'doggie bunny' for kangaroo and 'make a cup of tea' for kettle are examples. They also tend to attribute unusual meanings to words or phrases, because of the context in which they first heard them, such as the boy who thought that the Middle Ages was a time when everyone was middle-aged and the girl who thought a pinafore dress was a garment you wore at a performance of Gilbert and Sullivan's opera *H.M.S. Pinafore*.

Verbs present a problem because of the way they change in the past and future tenses. Most of the children speak in the present tense all the time, and only the ones who learn to speak really well are able to use tenses properly. If an autistic child reaches the stage when he realises that the ending 'ing' is added to make a word describing a present action, he will apply it indiscriminately, perhaps making this mistake for many years. He will describe a picture of a man smoking a pipe as 'Daddy piping' or one of a child blowing bubbles as 'Boy bubbling'.

The ability to pronounce words varies from one child to another. Some have little trouble, and others seem to be unable to make the necessary sounds. It is best not to discourage the child from talking by paying too much attention to his pronunciation too early on. A special problem for autistic children is controlling the pitch and lilt of the voice to make it sound natural and not mechanical. A co-operative child will try to imitate the correct intonation but this practice seems to make little difference to his spontaneous speech. There is some tendency to improvement with maturity.

Reversal of pronouns makes an autistic child's speech sound odd. Once the child speaks fairly well and is not discouraged by correction, it is worth while getting him to imitate the correct phrasing. At first you will need to help him with the whole sentence ('Can *I* have a biscuit') but after a time the smallest cue can be given in a whisper, and will be sufficient to help the child say the words correctly.

The small linking words are another source of difficulty. Constant practice in everyday situations can help especially if you make use of those that interest the child. He is more likely to learn the meaning of 'in' if you say 'The dinner is *in* the oven', than if you use the word 'in' in a context that has little significance for him. His favourite possession can be placed on or under or behind a chair so that he can learn the words for positions. The teaching should be arranged to amuse the child and should stop if he becomes bored or irritable.

Autistic children often try to say things but produce the wrong words in the wrong order. They also tend to cut the number of words to the bare minimum as with the child who said 'rom-a-beans' which was eventually found to mean, 'I want to have my baked beans on toast in the sitting-room so that I can watch television while I eat'. Parents need endless patience to sort out the muddle, but this is a worth-while exercise. The children can become unhappy and discouraged if they do their best to speak and people misunderstand, become impatient, or take no notice. One girl of eleven liked to talk to people but had little verbal skill. She had made something out of her constructional toy which she showed to a visitor, saying 'Hang-it-up'. The visitor was bewildered and could not carry on the conversation, but the child's mother knew that the model represented a duffle coat on a coat-hanger, and could admire it appropriately. However, she could not make up for the visitor's lack of appreciation as she saw from her daughter's sad face. Parents have to act as interpreters so that the children can make contact with people outside the family.

The children can be taught to answer simple questions, by making them part of a game. If they know the names of common animals, the game can begin with father (or mother) saying 'The cow says moo' – the moo being said in a way that amuses the child. The next stage is for father to say 'What does the cow say?' and then answer his own question 'The cow says moo'. This can be repeated several times while the child's interest is maintained. Then the 'moo' is left off the answer, and with luck the child will supply it himself. If not, then father must continue repeating the sequence and try again later. After several sessions of this kind the child will come to supply the whole answer. Each session should be a game and stopped before it bores the child. Other similar questions can be practised, remembering to go back to the earlier ones from time to time.

Carrying simple messages is a useful skill. A child can be taught to tell his father, 'Dinner's ready, Daddy'. To begin with, he has to practise repeating the words. It is no use starting with the instruction to 'Tell Daddy that dinner's ready' because the child will echo the whole sentence as he hears it. When he can say 'Dinner's ready, Daddy' well enough, he can be taken to his father and encouraged, by whispered cues, to give the message. Father (who should be well versed in his part too) says something like 'All right – Daddy coming', and everyone should show the child how well he has done. This needs to be repeated over and over again at every dinner-time, until the child can carry the message by himself. Eventually it may be possible to ask the child to 'Tell Daddy that dinner is ready', but this depends on how far his general skill with language develops.

In the early stages it may be difficult for an autistic child to express a preference if he is asked to choose one of two or more things. If you say to him, 'Do you want an apple or an orange?', he may repeat the whole sentence, or else echo the last word ('orange') even if he really preferred the apple. It is easier for him to make a choice if he can see the alternatives and touch the one he wants. If you encourage him to put his choice into words at the same time (for example, by saying 'Apple, please') he will eventually learn what to say.

Many young autistic children develop the habit of saying 'No' automatically, when they are asked to make too many choices. Part of this may be due to the frustration produced by their limited understanding, but the mischievous pleasure to be gained from annoying mother may keep the habit going. There is little point in asking the child 'Do you want some toast?' or 'Do you want milk or cocoa? or 'Do you want some potato?' at every single mealtime, to take a common example. The child should be given his meal, in the calm expectation that he will eat it. The opportunity to choose should be arranged only when you have the time to teach him how to make the correct reply, and you are sure that he understands the situation well enough to answer sensibly.

As with all other children, autistic children learn to say 'No' before 'Yes'. Questions are answered by repeating the words of the questioner, and a child may not say 'Yes' until he is eight or nine or even older. When he finally does learn, he then tends to answer 'Yes' to all questions regardless of the correct reply. The proper use of 'Yes' and 'No' can be taught by asking a series of very simple questions and prompting the correct answer: 'Is your coat blue?' – 'No'. 'Is your coat green?' – 'No'. 'Is your coat brown?' – 'Yes'. Constant practice is necessary before a child can be relied upon to use the words appropriately.

Polite phrases are a useful acquisition. 'Please' and 'Thank you' can be taught by patient insistence and by suitable prompting. The child should know that he will not be given the things he wants unless he says 'Please'. 'Thank you' has first of all to be said while both you and the child together are still holding on to the desired object, so that you can release it to him only when he has said the words. In time the words will become automatic. All this may seem a lot of effort for a useless convention, but it is worth while because it affects outsiders' opinion of the child and makes him acceptable in company. It is also sensible to teach him to say 'Can I have . . .?' instead of shouting a single word. Taking things without snatching is to be encouraged. Each family has to consider the conventions of its own circle and teach the child accordingly.

Every handicapped child who may wander should have his name and address sewn to his clothes. An autistic child who can speak can learn to give his name and address if his pronunciation is reasonable. He should be taught to give it in response to many different phrases ('What is your name?', 'Where do you live?', 'Who are you?', etc.) because you cannot guarantee how he will be asked if the need arises.

It is no use pretending that talking to a child with a severe language handicap is at all easy. Attempts at conversation are laborious in the extreme and often consist of repetitions of the same simple questions and answers. One common problem is that the children become resistant to change in the things they say and may repeat the same phrase or ask the same question over and over again. The best way to deal with this is to ignore the repeated phrases, but to encourage new verbal ideas and reward them with attention and interest.

Gestures and miming are used by normal people to aid communication, and autistic children need to be encouraged to use them. They can be taught to point at things accurately instead of using a vague wave of the arm. They may also enjoy a game of pretending to do everyday actions such as brushing hair, drinking from a cup, driving a car and so on. They find these things difficult and will need patient help if they are to learn to perform even the simplest mimed actions.

iii *Toys and games*

Autistic children do not play like normal children because their handicaps prevent or severely retard the development of imagination.

Parents can help the children gain useful experience by providing the toys that usually interest babies and toddlers and showing the children how to 'play' with them. They should be encouraged to handle the nesting boxes, coloured blocks, posting boxes and so on which give the children some experience of shape, size and colour and the relationship between one object and another. Their hands need to be guided to help them fit small boxes into large ones, or to build towers of blocks. The 'play' will cease as soon as adult supervision is removed, so it is a good idea for a parent to set aside a few short periods of time each day to work with the child. Many toy-making firms give the age ranges for which various toys are suitable, and it is useful to follow these stages in the right sequence, although the children are likely to be several years behind the normal development.

Later on many autistic children enjoy jigsaw puzzles. There are some excellent types of constructional toy on the market. If a child tends to avoid tasks involving much muscular effort, you can find constructional sets which are easily fitted together. You can also find sets which are suitable for children who are not very dextrous with their fingers.

There are now many toys which link words, sounds and pictures and some of these are ideal for a child with a language problem. In general, toys should be chosen which do not need complicated language or imagination for their enjoyment.

Autistic children have as much trouble in playing with other children as they do in playing with toys on their own. Unless they make unusually good progress they are unable to understand the purpose behind any game. They are not driven by a desire to win because they cannot grasp the concept of 'winning' with all the social awareness which this implies. By the time they are five or six years old it may be possible for parents to teach them simple games such as throwing and catching a ball which can later be played with other children. The problems of muscle control make even such a simple game difficult for an autistic child. If one adult stands behind the child, holding his arms and guiding him to catch and throw, he will eventually learn. A fairly large ball is better than a small one.

Hide-and-seek can be played when the child has sufficient understanding to know that objects still exist even if they are hidden away. It is best to begin by playing with one of the child's favourite possessions. One adult can cover the child's eyes or take him out of the room, while the other does the hiding. The child will need to be helped to search, and the object will have to be 'found' quickly at first, to avoid upsetting him by failure. As he begins to see the point, and to enjoy the surprise element, the game can go on longer and he can be encouraged to search for himself. He will tend to go back to the same place over and over again, and he will need cues to take him to other possible hiding places.

Most of the very simple games enjoyed by young children can be adapted to include an autistic child. The experience is particularly valuable if other children can join in but they need to be fairly mature in order to control their own behaviour enough to fit in with the needs of the handicapped child.

Drawing and painting are creative activities to be encouraged, but the children may have to be shown how to use pencils and paint by guiding their hands. They will begin by smearing and eating the paint until they reach a level of maturity at which they are interested in the marks they make on the paper rather than the feel of the materials. Even then many of them have little skill. It is the exceptional child who has any real ability in painting and drawing, but many of the children learn to enjoy trying to make pictures or colourful patterns.

Some autistic children are late in understanding that

pictures can represent objects. One child was interested only while a picture was being drawn for her and looked away as soon as the pencil ceased moving on the paper. Another had to be shown real objects together with the pictures of them before she understood that the one represented the other. Books with plain clear pictures of everyday things are best. Cartoons and pictures with fussy detail are not much use.

The hardest problem is to keep up the autistic child's interest in any activity. A normal child plays as naturally as he breathes because his understanding of the world is always a step or so ahead of his physical achievements. He is always reaching out to anticipate the next stage of complexity. The autistic child is held back by his lack of comprehension of what life is about, and he needs constant adult supervision and encouragement to prevent him returning to his preoccupation with simple sensations.

iv *Social manners and social relationships*

Gestures and facial expressions are important in social communication. All autistic children have difficulties with this kind of language, and some of them are so handicapped that their faces appear wooden and expressionless in almost all situations. Normal people are used to estimating the feelings of others from their expressions, and often assume that autistic children are without any emotions at all. Faced with a child of this kind, most people soon give up the effort to produce a visible response, and a vicious circle is created, since the child cannot initiate contact for himself.

It is well worth while for parents to try to teach the children the outward expressions of their inner feelings. A child can be taught to shake hands if his hand is guided correctly whenever a visitor offers his hand first. It is better to teach this as a response to a proffered hand rather than encouraging the child to make the first move, since he will not understand when it is correct to do this and when not.

Positive signs of affection within the family can also be taught. Instead of allowing the child to accept a hug and a kiss passively, his own arms can be guided to return the hug. He can also be taught to hold on properly with his arms and legs when he is picked up and carried by an adult, instead of lying limply like a rag doll. Kissing can be taught in the same way, by gently guiding the child's head. If he just touches his lips on the other person's cheek, that is good enough to start with. Again it is best for the child to learn this as a response to affection from others. Once the children grasp the idea, they usually come to enjoy these social contacts, and might easily assume that this was the way to greet everyone.

Even though it may sound rather odd, one can teach a child to smile by moving the corners of his lips. When he reaches the stage of development in which he is responsive to such teaching (perhaps around six to seven years of age, but earlier in some and later in others) parents can demonstrate different expressions on their own faces, and tell him the names, such as 'smile' and 'frown'. They can use the appropriate tone of voice, or link the names with the emotions – 'smile-happy' 'frown-angry'. A session in which the child's face is moulded into expressions while he watches a mirror can be helpful. Pictures of people with different expressions can be compared and named. The children often find this highly diverting, and laugh uproariously at their own and their parents' funny faces, and this gives the lessons a happy and positive atmosphere.

An autistic child's bodily postures or way of walking may emphasise the fact that he is handicapped. This can be corrected to some extent. He can be encouraged to swing his arms as he walks and to stand up straight without having his arms bent at the elbows or his head on one side. Sometimes the children tend to hold their mouths open, and this should be discouraged if possible. Helping to overcome these problems needs much patience and good humour. The odd postures and movements are in large part due to their immature development so the children have to try hard to stand and walk well. Irritable nagging from parents will cause justifiable resentment.

By the time a child is six or seven years old he may be able to learn to look at people instead of through or past them. This tends to come naturally with increasing age, but can be encouraged. It may be necessary to start with sessions in which his father or mother gently holds the child's head, and attracts his visual attention. The way to success is to obtain a child's co-operation by making faces that amuse him, or whispering, or singing a favourite song. In short the teaching should be pleasant for the child. One game that often makes a child laugh while encouraging him to look in your eyes is to touch noses and then twist your head so that a funny visual effect is created by the way your eyes move.

The children's interest in other people grows with experience. Friends and relations can help especially if the child's handicaps are explained to them. People who regularly call at the door are often friendly and understanding. The child can be taught to answer the door when told and to say 'Hallo'. (If you live in an area where not all callers are desirable it is best to teach him not to answer the door automatically when the bell rings, but to wait for your instructions.)

It is easier for these children to relate to adults than to other children, especially those of the same age or younger. This is probably because adults are able to adapt themselves to the child, whereas other children do not have the necessary insight, and do not modify their behaviour. The exceptions are some normal children who have a handicapped brother and sister of their own. If the situation is handled well by their parents, they may be remarkably good at interacting with an autistic child. There is not much that parents can do to make it easier for their autistic child to get on better with other children, except to help him join in with simple games. Most autistic children with moderate or severe handicaps will always need adult supervision and guidance whenever they are with a group of normal children. The situation must never be allowed to degenerate so that the autistic child becomes aggressive, or else withdraws and wanders away on his own. He must be protected against the occasional normal child who reacts to a handicapped person by bullying and teasing. Autistic children cannot defend themselves and do not learn to do so through experience. They have neither the verbal wit nor the physical skills to hold their own among their peers.

So far I have concentrated upon ways of encouraging social mixing. The other side of the picture can be seen in some children who make good progress. They may become over-friendly and sociable, in an immature way, and fail to discriminate between people they know and complete strangers. One girl of ten, who had had quite severe visual as well as speech handicaps, tended to assume that people she met in the street were people she knew. She would rush up to them with a joyful greeting, to their utter amazement. Her parents had to restrain her and explain many times over that she must not talk to people in the street unless her parents made the first move. She was most upset at first, but the phase passed after a few months. There is no easy answer, since one naturally does not want to discourage a spontaneous friendliness which one has spent so long in encouraging. However, I have not met any children who have become withdrawn again because of their over-friendliness has had to be curbed.

v *Outings and social occasions*

When they are under four or five years old, autistic children, especially those with marked visual problems, tend to find crowds and bustle confusing and frightening.

This makes it difficult to take them into shops, to parties or even into crowded streets. As they grow older and their handicaps lessen, most of the children begin to enjoy outings, especially since they have so little creative play with which to occupy themselves.

In the transition stage, when fear is receding and enjoyment is growing, expeditions should be carefully planned. First of all you should arrange to keep them fairly short, and not too far from home, so that you can easily remove the child if the situation proves too much for him. You have to try different kinds of outing. If one is not a success, then leave it for a while and try again later. A visit to the zoo, with lively, noisy, smelly animals, may terrify an autistic child of three, but give great pleasure to one of seven years.

With a young child a certain amount of equipment is necessary. Food may have to be taken if a restaurant is a problem because hunger can make a child more difficult to manage. A pot may be necessary if public lavatories frighten the child. A damp sponge and a towel or paper tissues are invaluable aids. A favourite toy, or small object which does not look too odd to strangers, should be allowed, to give the child a link with his home. The most important preparation of all is basic training in reasonable social manners, so that parents can feel relaxed, and the whole family, including the child, can enjoy the outing.

Later on, outings can become longer and more complicated. It helps the child to tell him in advance (in simple words) and to draw pictures of where he is going and what will happen. Most theatre and film shows are of no interest to autistic children, but they may enjoy musicals where much of the action is singing and dancing, with few spoken lines. Their pleasure is considerably increased if they can hear a record of the music before they see the show, so that they can learn the tunes. Cartoon films with music are usually a success. If the child can attend private film shows first it is easier to teach him that he must not talk or wander around during the performance. The children may be delighted to join in with clapping and laughing even though they do not understand the joke. Their humour tends to be concrete. Slapstick comedy with people falling over and throwing water around goes down well, so some old silent films will appeal.

Older autistic children usually like to go to parties although they may join in very little. One boy was sad when his sisters were invited to parties without him. The hosts had not realised that in his own quiet way he was enjoying himself. Parents, who so often have to stand between the world and their child, need to overcome any diffidence they feel, and explain to friends and relations, so that the child has as much social life as possible.

vi *Travel and holidays*

Once past the difficult early years, and once special fears of buses, cars or trains have been overcome, many autistic children thoroughly enjoy travelling. Some parents even find that their children behave better on a journey than on any other occasion.

Apart from the actual journey, holidays may be difficult. A young autistic child may be bewildered by new surroundings, and may never settle during the whole period away from home. Many families do not take a vacation, or else try to arrange temporary residential care for the child while the rest of the family goes away.

This problem can often be overcome with time and patience. Careful teaching of social behaviour and basic co-operation and obedience eventually enables the family to live a more normal life. The most easily managed type of holiday (apart from staying with an understanding friend or relative) is to rent a small house or chalet for the family, away from other people, and to cater for oneself. Some of the autistic child's favourite possessions should be taken to make him feel secure. The days can be planned to include some activity to keep him amused and happy.

When a child is reasonably well behaved, staying a night in a hotel can be tried. Once this is accomplished other kinds of holidays become possible. Some parents have taken their children abroad and the whole family has benefited from the experience. The same rules apply whatever expedition is planned. These are: be consistent and firm in social training; prepare the child in advance through words and pictures; increase the scope of the expeditions gradually (that is, don't move from one afternoon in the local park straight to three weeks in a hotel in Italy); and take his favourite clothes and toys with you to preserve the child's link with the familiar and the secure.

vii *Memory and anticipation – the practical use of pictures, reading and writing*

Autistic children have difficulty in grasping the concept of time. The meanings of the words 'minutes', 'hours', 'days', 'weeks' or 'yesterday', 'tomorrow', 'next year' are hard to understand and to learn. This affects the children's social behaviour in different ways at different stages of development. In the early years the problem shows itself as an inability to wait. This is common to all young children, but, as usual, it goes on much longer in an autistic child. Some of them begin to scream if made to wait more than a second for their food, for a walk, a ride in the car or anything else that they want. An orderly routine reduces the occasions on which this happens, but the children can be taught, in gradual stages, to wait in moderate patience. It is easier to do this once the child pays some attention to words. When he is seated in his special chair for dinner you can say to him 'Dinner in a minute' or 'Dinner soon' or whatever phrase you would use naturally, as long as it is fairly short. You wait a few seconds and then give him his food. The waiting time can be lengthened very slowly, always using the phrase which reassures him that dinner really *is* just coming. Once a child has learnt to wait for a while he is easier to take out, and into other people's homes.

The lack of understanding of time also shows itself in an inability to consider the past or to anticipate the future. Parents often say how sad it is that their children do not seem to recall happy events, or look forward to enjoyable occasions, because this means they lack two of the major sources of pleasure in life. The children can be helped to overcome this handicap, at home and at school, if regular events that they enjoy are planned and talked about, before and after they have occurred. The events, which can be small and simple like having something extra nice for tea, should be arranged frequently enough for the child to be able to remember.

Pictures and diagrams are invaluable in this connection, once the children's visual understanding has reached an appropriate level. A calendar can be drawn, with each day represented by a square in a row of seven for one week. The name of each day can be written in, and then a little drawing of the central event of each day put into the square. The child can cross off yesterday's square (while you say 'yesterday all gone' or something similar), then the events of today can be described with the aid of the picture. Some children manage to grasp the idea of a day and a week, and then a whole month can be drawn. Events inside a day can be placed in time, 'before dinner', 'after dinner', 'before tea', and 'after tea' and so on. Later on, the words morning and afternoon and evening can be taught by linking them to meal times.

If a special outing is planned, pictures can be drawn to show what will happen, using the appropriate words at the same time. Photographs or, better still, slides which can be projected on to a screen, can be taken on holidays, or trips to the seaside, and these can be shown to the child afterwards and the story told in simple words. It is a good idea to have pictures or slides of each member of the family, friends, and household pets, so that the child can look at them and name them.

In general an autistic child can learn more from a picture than from words, because, almost always, the difficulties of visual understanding are less severe and improve faster than those of auditory comprehension. The children find it hard to follow a sequence of events and here a diagram can be invaluable. One girl was told that she was going out shopping with mother, then to a restaurant and finally to a film show. She repeated this sequence time and time again, each time getting it wrong. It is not at all surprising that children with this problem become anxious, and go on and on worrying about it until they get it right. Finally this little girl was shown a picture with the shop at the top, the restaurant underneath, and the cinema under that, and her finger was guided to touch each one in turn in the correct sequence. This satisfied her completely. (It would not have worked if she had still been in the stage in which left-right, back-front and up-down were hopelessly confused.) A boy of ten was helped to understand words like second, minute, hour and day when his mother drew lines of different length to demonstrate the relationship of the different time periods.

A fair number of autistic children learn to read, in the sense that they can pronounce words they see written down, but hardly any of them have much comprehension of reading material. They therefore do not read for pleasure or interest. One way parents at home can help a child to feel that reading can be worth the effort is to prepare a book of 'stories' about the child's own everyday life, illustrated with drawings or photographs. It can be as simple as one sentence on each page. 'Tom get up', 'Tom eating breakfast', 'Tom going to shop with Mummy', each with its own picture. A seaside holiday book can be made in the same way.

The same idea applies when encouraging a child to practise writing. An autistic girl of twelve began to enjoy writing words when she realised that she could make a list of the things she wanted when shopping. Developing this skill then helped her in another way. She became tense and anxious for several days before a special event because she hated waiting. Then she began to write down a few words about whatever event she was anticipating. This seemed to reassure her that it really would happen in the end, and she was able to relax and look forward with pleasure.

Normal children enjoy bedtime stories before settling down to sleep. Autistic children do not understand language well enough to appreciate fiction, but they often do enjoy it if mother or father goes over the events of the day. A 'story' of this kind, perhaps followed by a favourite song, makes a cosy family routine with which to say good night, as well as helping the development of language and memory.

PHYSICAL HEALTH

Lack of speech makes it difficult for an autistic child to show when he does not feel well, or to indicate the site of any pain. Parents have to observe his behaviour as carefully as they can, and notice any signs of illness such as extra fretfulness, lack of appetite, lethargy, rashes or a feverish flush. It is useful to teach a child a few words that he can use if he is in pain or discomfort. 'Throat sore' or 'leg hurt', give some guide to what is wrong. A small girl liked to have an adhesive plaster put on any minor injury, and when she had an attack of tonsillitis the first sign was that she said to her mother, 'Poor froat – put plaster on.'

Many autistic children furiously resist attempts at physical examination. It is possible to overcome this by playing a game of 'examining like a doctor' so that the child becomes accustomed to a hand on his tummy and the bell of a stethoscope on his chest. It also helps to practise opening and closing the eyes and the mouth when told (the words 'close' and 'open' are often confused by the children). If possible, the child should get to know the family doctor as a friend before he has any physical illness, so that he is less apprehensive when he does need treatment.

Handicapped children who have problems with chewing and with mouth and tongue movements are particularly liable to tooth decay. They are given much soft food, and they do not use their tongues to remove scraps of food from between their teeth. Careful and regular toothbrushing is essential. An electric toothbrush if used properly cleans effectively, and also helps the child to become used to the feeling of vibration, which is similar to that of some dental instruments. Regular visits to the dentist are necessary, and should begin well before any treatment is needed. A dentist needs patience and a way with children which will enable him to teach an autistic child to sit in the chair and allow his teeth to be inspected and cleaned. Some children become so used to dental procedures that they will accept small fillings without an anaesthetic. Others, however, will need a general anaesthetic for such procedures.

If an autistic child has to go into hospital it is better for him if his mother can accompany him. He needs her reassurance and comfort even more than a normal child of the same age. The doctors and nurses will need the mother's help. She can explain things to the child and tell him what he has to do. She can also tell the staff of her child's needs since he usually cannot convey his meaning to strangers. The doctor and ward sister may appreciate some information about autistic children if they have not treated a child of this kind before.* In this situation a mother has to hide her natural anxiety, present a calm and confident front to her child, and co-operate fully with the medical and nursing staff, so that the child feels as happy and relaxed as possible.

*The British National Society for Autistic Children publishes a brief information leaflet for this purpose.

A doctor or dentist who is treating a child should be told if he is receiving any drugs, such as sleeping tablets or daytime sedatives. This is particularly important if an anaesthetic (local or general) has to be given. Autistic children may be muddled and confused when they wake up from an anaesthetic, and may need a sedative to calm them down. They will be helped and comforted if a parent or another familiar person is there to give reassurance.

Among the drugs which may be given to autistic children to lessen overactive and difficult behaviour there are some which make the skin sensitive to sunlight. This may cause swelling and a rash if the child spends any time in the sunshine. This can be prevented by avoiding the sun, and wearing long sleeves and a shady hat. Your doctor will tell you if any tablets he gives your child are likely to have this effect, and he will advise on special precautions.

PROBLEMS OF ADOLESCENCE

These depend upon how much progress each individual child has made by the time he has reached the years of adolescence. At one end of the scale, some children change so little that they still have the same problems as those of the young autistic child. At the other end, some children are able to talk and understand fairly well and their difficulties have something in common with those of the normal teenager.

i *Immature social responses*

I have already mentioned this problem in various sections of this book. The extra difficulty presented in adolescence is that the immature behaviour and naive comments attract far more attention in someone who is physically almost adult than they do in a younger child. Parents have to continue to teach general rules of conduct, and also the applications of these rules to any particular situation. They can arrange suitable opportunities for social mixing with other normal adolescents who are sensible and understanding. Suitable companions have to be chosen with some care, because some normal adolescents of a mischievous turn of mind could take advantage of an autistic child's naive innocence and passivity, and lead him into trouble.

Because of their immaturity, most autistic adolescents do not have the feelings of rebellion against their parents which are seen in normal young people. They do not go in for demonstrations, for drug-taking, for peculiar forms of dress, or any of the outward signs of protest. The usual complaint of parents of an autistic adolescent is that he has very little drive to do anything. Children who have been overactive often become underactive in their adolescent years. When rebelliousness does occur it is likely to be a childish irritability and stubbornness, rather than a determined, sustained protest. This can be trying to manage, and it is not easy to combine the necessary patience and understanding of the teenager's handicaps with an attempt to treat him as much like an adult as is possible in view of his limitations and need for protection and security. A desire to be independent may come in adult life to some people who have been autistic as children, and who have developed enough to have some concept of what independence means. When this happens, all that the parents can do is to allow their son or daughter to make the experiment of living away from home, but to be ready to give whatever help is necessary if things go wrong, without appearing to be over-protective.

ii *Sexual development*

Puberty is usually not delayed in autistic children, even though they often look younger than their actual age. Interest in sex tends to be on an immature level. Some of the children develop a childish curiosity about their own and other people's bodies, and may innocently try to undress other children. The fact that this is 'not done' is one more of the rules which they have to learn.

Masturbation can be a problem in autistic children. Their lack of social sense may mean that they masturbate in public, especially if they are unoccupied and bored. This should be discouraged in the same way as any other socially undesirable behaviour, not because masturbation is in any way harmful, but because other people do not accept a child who behaves in this way.

Menstruation usually begins within the same age range as with normal girls. Special waterproof plastic covers for sanitary pads can be bought. A routine for changing pads regularly should be followed until the girl can cope for herself. Sometimes an autistic child will talk about her periods to people she meets. Although it is an excellent idea to adopt an open and matter-of-fact attitude towards the facts of life, nevertheless it is necessary to teach a child discretion in these matters because there are still many people who are shocked or embarrassed by these subjects. You can explain that the time to make comments or ask questions is when alone with Mother, and not when other people are around.

Asking questions about conception and birth presupposes a reasonable level of language development, so it is only a small minority of autistic adolescents who will even ask their parents about these matters. Answers should be frank, but simple enough for the child's understanding. A few adolescents may say that they intend to get married and have children, but people who have been autistic as children rarely seem to have any drive towards finding a regular boy or girl friend, or towards adult sexual activity, although they may show a naive preference and physical affection for the opposite sex. In any case they almost always lack the social skills to attract another boy or girl. Some parents worry because their autistic daughter is over-friendly to strangers, and is easily led. Usually, however, it is fairly easy to supervise such a child, and her social contacts. One or two cases have been reported (without much documentary evidence) of people with autistic behaviour as children who grew up and married, but they seem to have grown out of the symptoms completely by the time of adolescence. In these circumstances it is difficult to know if they really did have early childhood autism.

iii *Insight*

It is difficult to know how far young autistic children are aware of their handicaps. They certainly feel intense distress and unhappiness when they are frustrated or confused by their environment, but whether or not they compare themselves with other children is difficult to estimate. It is unlikely that the majority of the children can do this because they are limited by their language handicap. Sometimes, however, an autistic child will stand on the edge of a group of normal children and watch their play with a look of wistful longing and intense sadness.

The children who show marked improvement are likely to have a fair amount of insight by the time they reach adolescence. They may express this in their own way. One boy used to say sadly, over and over again, 'Can't do it. Got no brain.' A girl of fourteen who was able to talk well once asked her mother, 'Mummy, when God made me, why didn't he make me quite right?' Other children ask why they are different from their brothers and sisters. When an autistic adolescent begins to think about this problem he may become miserable and depressed. He will need comfort and reassurance from his parents and family. It will also help him to point out the things that he can do well, and to explain that everyone has problems and handicaps.

Occasionally an adolescent who is concerned about his handicaps will try to do something to show that he is normal, and this may have disastrous results. One young man thought he would improve his health if he took up running, so he ran for miles in bitterly cold weather in his vest and pants, and was found in an exhausted condition a very long way from home. It may not be possible to predict, and therefore prevent, this kind of impulsive behaviour. It is also impossible to shield a bright autistic adolescent from the knowledge that he is not the same as others. What one can do is to offer continued affection and concern, and to help him find some occupation which can give him the feeling that he has a role in life.

iv *Employment problems*

A small number of autistic adults manage to work in open employment. The occupations they have followed cover a wide range and include work in mathematics, office work, piano-tuning, bricklaying, street-cleaning and domestic work. In every case a sympathetic and knowledgeable employer was the most important factor in allowing the person to settle down into a routine. There are a number of problems which can cause difficulties in finding suitable employment. The language disorder excludes work which involves good conversational ability, social interaction or high skill in reading. The lack of flexibility means that work where instructions are complicated and methods change frequently is likely to be unsuitable. Some autistic adults may still be sensitive to noises and bright lights and may be unable to tolerate these conditions in a factory. They tend to be upset if people are impatient or irritable, or if anyone shouts loudly. When they start work they need someone to explain every little detail, to show them the cloakroom and toilets, how to collect lunch from the canteen, what time to stop work and so on, and someone to keep an eye open to make sure everything goes smoothly. The journey to work may have unexpected snags. With public transport there is the risk that the usual bus or train may be late or cancelled, and this may produce confusion and distress. A parent, hostel warden or other guardian usually has to make sure that an autistic adult looks after himself, has regular meals, and changes his clothes as often as is necessary.

On the positive side, those who can fit into open employment are hard-working and conscientious. Once they have learned the rules they apply them with meticulous accuracy. (This can have its negative side, since striving for perfect accuracy may slow up the work below a level which is acceptable.) They are completely honest and open, and usually popular with their colleagues, once their handicaps are understood and accepted.

The majority of autistic adults need sheltered conditions, in which a wide range of work is available so that a suitable job can be found to fit each individual person's special skills. Some people with experience of the problems of employing autistic adolescents recommend that work should be organised to allow a change of task several times during the day, to avoid boredom. Many of the more handicapped autistic adults need much supervision and repetition of instructions to keep them working, because lethargy and lack of initiative is a major problem. The effort to provide occupation is well worth while because constructive activity makes the odd behaviour less obvious, and encourages continued improvement.

THE MOST DIFFICULT CHILDREN

i *Sub-groups*

Since I wrote the first edition of this book, I have watched many autistic children grow up. Some have improved slowly but surely and life has become much easier for them and their families. This does not happen to them all. Some make little or no useful progress even though they have been given loving care and good, special education.

This lack of progress tends to occur mainly in two kinds of children. First, there are those who have no understanding or use of language and few or no skills even after two or three years of appropriate education. Often, children in this group have autistic features, rather than classic autism, and they score in the severely or profoundly retarded range on psychological tests.

Second, there are autistic children, often with the classic syndrome, who have the ability to learn a variety of non-verbal, even verbal tasks, but who have no interest in or a marked objection to using these skills for any practical purpose. This type of child usually has limited language comprehension, even if he has a fairly large vocabulary of words, and has absolutely no development of imaginative activities. He has no idea of the purpose of the things he is taught, and sees no reason to carry out repeatedly meaningless and therefore boring activities. These children do not have enough desire to please other people for this to motivate them, neither will they passively accept direction from others.

Applying pressure to make them learn produces little useful result and may, especially in the second group of children, lead to temper tantrums, negativism, aggression towards others, or self-injury. The lack of constructive pursuits means that they fill the empty hours with simple, stereotyped, repetitive routines.

ii *Organising activities*

Once it becomes clear that little educational progress is likely, then effort should be turned to organising activities that are enjoyable for the child or adult concerned, and that reduce, as far as possible, the tendency to difficult behaviour. The types of activities likely to be acceptable to adults of this kind, as well as children, are listening to music, moving to music, sand and water play, the physical exercise and experiences provided by the very large foam-rubber-filled or inflatable shapes specially made for handicapped people, electronic devices that produce a wide range of visual, auditory and tactile sensations, outdoor pursuits such as walking, coach rides, picnics, paddling and swimming. Tricycles, swings, see-saws and roundabouts and similar equipment are all useful. Horse-riding supervised by instructors who are experienced with handicapped people often proves to be a special pleasure.

Some teaching should continue, but should concentrate upon the most practical details of self-care – toilet training, feeding, dressing and washing. If a child enjoys some aspect of more usual school work, such as making jig-saw puzzles, then this can be encouraged, but too much pressure is unhelpful and can be positively harmful for this kind of child.

The daily programme needs to be organised in detail and in advance so that there is plenty of variety, no waiting around doing nothing, and no activity is continued for longer than the child can be expected to show interest. The timing can be worked out from observation of the children's reactions. It is considerably easier to cope with small groups with a staff ratio of around one to three. Plenty of space indoors and outdoors, and quiet places for individual sessions, are also most desirable.

iii *Managing aggression*

Some autistic people who make little progress are never aggressive, but in others it can be a major problem. The conditions in which it usually occurs should be observed and an attempt made to understand the reason so that outbursts can be avoided. The cause can be as trivial as a sudden noise of a particular pitch, or the fact that the favourite piece of string has been mislaid.

If aggression involving another child does occur, they should be separated as quickly as possible, but with the minimum of fuss. Removal to a room alone but under unobtrusive supervision for a time may be helpful. Some autistic people dislike proximity to others so much that they see isolation as a reward. If this is the case, much difficulty can be avoided if the space available is organised carefully.

In schools or other units, staff should agree on the action to be taken as soon as aggressive behaviour begins, and should work together as a team. Minor and physically harmless aggression towards members of staff is best ignored, but more serious attacks have to be restrained. Confidence is all-important for successful management. It is harder for parents at home, especially for the mother when she is on her own with a child who is too big for her to control physically. Avoiding trouble may be the only method she can use, but this can lead to all kinds of problems if the autistic person learns how to manipulate the situation. Aggressive behaviour, especially towards younger brothers or sisters, is a major reason for parents looking for residential care. Medication sometimes helps, but it is a question of trial and error, with no guarantee of success.

Self-directed aggression – that is, self-injury such as hand-biting, head-banging, or face-scratching – can be especially severe in these children. Methods of dealing with the milder forms have already been mentioned (see page 94), but a further note is necessary concerning the more serious and long-lasting problems. The method of management using some form of unpleasant physical experience or physical restraint as discouragement is, in my experience, of little help in the long term, even if it appears to succeed for a time. After a while, the method of discouraging the behaviour may, from the child's point of view, come to be an integral part of the whole pattern of self-injury and, therefore, no longer an effective deterrent.

The ideal solution is to find a more enjoyable alternative occupation and to pay as little attention as possible to the self-injuring behaviour. But this ideal solution is often not possible in practice. In these cases protective clothing such as special helmets, gloves or one-piece suits may have to be used. Much ingenuity is needed to design the clothing so that it interferes as little as possible with movement and the possibility of engaging in more constructive activities. It should be removed at any time when self-injury is unlikely to occur, for example during mealtimes. Tranquillising medication is often prescribed, but this reduces the general level of activity without having any specific effect on the undesirable behaviour.

iv *Coping at home*

It is clearly very hard for parents to manage these difficult children at home, especially as they grow older, bigger and stronger. The kind of daily programme suggested here needs the resources of a school or other centre and no parent would be able to occupy the child for all his waking hours during the evenings, weekends or holidays when he is at home. At these times, a compromise is necessary. For the sake of the rest of the family, for at least some of the time the autistic child has to be left to his repetitive activities, in his own room if he prefers this, as long as what he does is not dangerous or destructive, and if it keeps him quiet and peaceful. If the parents put aside some periods of time, even if only half-an-hour or so each day, when they do encourage him to take part in suitable activities, preferably involving all the family, this is often the best that can be done. It helps if plans for the holiday times can be made in advance, so that the problem of thinking what to do is dealt with all at once instead of being a daily chore.

HOME OR RESIDENTIAL CARE

All parents have to consider whether they should keep a handicapped child in the family, or try to place him in residential care. This question is likely to arise at various special times: in the early years when the fact that the child is handicapped first becomes clear, when other siblings are born, during adolescence – especially if there is a return to, or exacerbation of behaviour problems – and when parents are ill or becoming elderly and less able to cope.

A secure and loving family, together with the right school, can offer an autistic child the best possible environment in which he can develop whatever potential he may have. If the parents decide to keep the child at home, and the family is not experiencing an unacceptable degree of strain, they should be given every encouragement and help. There is nothing to be gained for the child from admission to a hospital unit, unless some special problem makes this necessary. Diagnosis and assessment should be carried out on an out-patient or day-patient basis unless there are good reasons necessitating a short period of admission. If the parents want the child to live at home, and things are going well, then education should be at a day school if at all possible. Weekly or termly boarding may have to be arranged if no suitable day place is available.

When making their decision, parents have to consider the rest of the family and themselves, as well as the handicapped child. There are many reasons why residential care might have to be found. One or other parent may have a chronic illness, there may be only one parent, the housing situation might make caring for a difficult child almost impossible. One of the most important reasons is that the problems caused by the autistic child are proving harmful to the physical or mental wellbeing of a brother, sister or parent. This is particularly likely to occur with the very difficult child whose behaviour does not improve despite the love and care of the family.

When the autistic child reaches adolescence, whether or not there are behaviour problems, thought has to be given to his future. If it seems likely he will remain dependent as an adult, then eventual residential placement should be carefully considered. The usual cycle of life in industrialised societies is that young adults move away from the family home and begin a life of their own. There is much to be said for handicapped people making the same move, but into a suitable sheltered setting. In any case, this will eventually happen when the parents can no longer cope, or die. If the move is made in early adult life, the separation can be made gradually rather than suddenly, the parents can still provide a home at weekends or for holidays, or else can visit regularly. They can also keep a close eye on the residential home or hospital, and work with other families to maintain or improve standards.

One important and often unconsidered aspect of caring for autistic adults is that their experience of the world differs in many ways from that of non-autistic people. The autistic person shares the same needs for food, warmth, and skilled and loving care, but he is unlikely to be affected by the beauty or ugliness of his surroundings, or the physical appearance or level of intelligence of those around him. The more difficult and severely handicapped group have little or no interest in being in the normal community. To them, space where they can walk and, for some of the time at least, make their odd, stereotyped movements without upsetting other people, is far more necessary. When considering the suitability of a residential centre, especially a mental handicap hospital, which may be the only placement available, parents should try to see the environment from the point of view of the autistic person and not judge it on the standards they would prefer for themselves. This is *not* a defence of all such hospitals as they are at the moment. Many, but not all, fall far below acceptable standards and much effort is needed to improve them. Nor is it an argument against developing new types of services. The point I wish to make is that the concept of a sheltered setting, where the behaviour of very severely handicapped and difficult people can be accepted, is useful and good, and is the right choice for some autistic adults, especially those for whom residential communities geared to constructive work apply too much pressure. Mental handicap hospitals have traditionally fulfilled such a function and will continue to do so in the foreseeable future.

In the end, it is the parents who have to look at all facets of the problem of home or residential care and make up their own minds. They should have the benefit of expert advice but the decision is theirs alone. When they have made the choice, they should be given all help possible to put the decision into effect. Residential care should be organised so that the family can maintain contact with their child and not feel that he no longer belongs to them. If a child or adult does have to live away from home, the parents should not regard this as a failure, but as an appropriate choice in the light of their family responsibilities.

10

The autistic child's family

THE PROBLEMS OF BROTHERS AND SISTERS

It is hard to find evidence of the effect on the brothers and sisters of having a handicapped child in the family. Some studies of different kinds of handicaps have been done, and have given conflicting results. It seems that some normal children are adversely affected by a handicapped sibling, whereas others manage well and perhaps benefit from the experience in the end. The effects are related to a whole series of definable and indefinable factors, including the severity of the child's handicaps and behaviour problems, the personalities of the brothers and sisters, and the attitudes of the parents.

Obviously, however brothers and sisters respond to the experience, they do face a number of special problems. Perhaps the hardest thing for them is that their parents have to give so much attention to the handicapped child (particularly one who is autistic) that the others do not have their fair share. This is worse for a child who is near in age to the autistic child, and parents have to be aware of this danger and do their best to give their normal children plenty of affection and interest. If it is possible to arrange for some domestic help, this may enable the parents to organise their time more easily.

An older normal child of school age, with a young autistic brother or sister, does not suffer quite so much from lack of attention, but he may feel unable to bring his friends home to play. It is easier for him if his parents encourage and welcome his friends (however tired and harassed they may feel) and make sure that there is somewhere where they can play in peace. It is best to explain frankly and simply about the child's handicaps and to answer the questions of the brothers and sisters and their friends in as calm and relaxed a manner as possible.

A destructive autistic child may break his brothers' and sisters' toys. Normal children naturally find this hard to bear. They need to have a special place to lock their precious possessions out of harm's way. Parents should teach their autistic child, as soon as they can, not to touch any toys except his own. They should replace all damaged toys if they possibly can. If a normal child is reassured that his rights are being respected, he will accept the occasional loss of a possession with better grace, and will be more willing to play with his autistic brother and help him to use toys.

A normal child may worry about the possibility of developing symptoms like his handicapped sibling. He will not understand why his brother or sister is different, and he may have all kinds of alarming fears and fantasies. Parents need to be sensitive to these feelings. They can help by their calm acceptance of all their children, their willingness to discuss and to explain, and their love and reassurance.

An adolescent may worry about the possibility of having an autistic child himself when he marries. Some facts are known about the chance of a recurrence of early childhood autism within a family. A few families have more than one autistic child, and in other cases a brother or a sister has some other mental or physical handicap. Sometimes there is a family history of left-handedness and difficulty with talking, reading or writing, or of mild eccentricity and lack of sociability. It seems that there is approximately a one-in-fifty chance of a sibling of an autistic child having the same handicap, compared with one in 2,000 for children in general. The exact risk must vary depending on the cause in the affected child, inherited factors being greater in some causes than others (see page 48). The risks for other relations are not known, but are likely to be less than for brothers and sisters.

Some normal children enjoy teaching an autistic child and can involve an autistic brother or sister in a variety of activities. It is also common to find that normal children with a handicapped sibling develop an air of maturity beyond their years. Parents have to beware of placing too much responsibility on the shoulders of their normal offspring, and make sure that they have plenty of time for ordinary childish pursuits, without having their play interrupted by the autistic child.

There is sometimes a tendency for parents, especially mothers, to respond to the helplessness of an autistic child by giving him preferential treatment. This feeling is understandable, but should be resisted. The normal children should not have to take second place to the one who is handicapped. The needs of everyone in the family must be respected and an attempt made to achieve an acceptable balance.

THE PROBLEMS OF PARENTS

Parents have to cope with a series of problems some of which are practical and some of which are emotional. Many of these are common to parents of mentally handicapped children in general, while others are special to the families of autistic children.

GENERAL PROBLEMS

The parents of any chronically handicapped child have to undergo a complete change of attitude when they first learn the truth, and this is a painful process. Like all parents they start off with the expectation that they have a normal baby who will grow up like everyone else. They have to adjust to the fact that all their hopes and plans for their child's future (and to some extent their own future as well) will have to be changed. It is hard for them to resist the feeling that somehow they have failed. Physical or mental abnormalities seem to trigger off feelings of shame and guilt which are quite irrational, but which have to be anticipated and understood.

The immediate practical problems with a mentally retarded child are those of greatly prolonged baby and toddler stages, often with problems of feeding and general health, plus difficult behaviour as well.

Once school age is reached, the parents see other children entering the normal school system, and their own child going to a special school. In some areas, these special units are referred to by unpleasant names by other children (and some adults) and the shame and sadness, which may have faded a little, come into the foreground again. School holidays are often a problem because the mother has to organise her day so that she can cope with a bored and difficult child as well as doing the housework.

Dependence on the parents usually continues into adolescence and adult life. Difficult behaviour becomes eventually less marked, but any tendency to aggressiveness is much harder to cope with in a fully grown adult than in a small child. Even if schooling was provided throughout childhood, a suitable occupation may be hard to find, especially if the handicaps are too severe to allow placement in open employment. Handicapped people are bored and miserable when unoccupied and their symptoms may become more obvious in these circumstances.

Parents always worry about what will happen after they die. If their handicapped child lives a limited but happy life at home, parents find it hard to bear the thought that he will pass the remainder of his days in an institution.

I have already mentioned the problems of the other normal children in a family, which naturally cause the parents concern. Other relatives may provide help and support, but sometimes their attitudes can be less constructive. They may feel that a handicapped child brings shame on the whole family (disregarding the fact that all families have handicapped relatives somewhere in their histories). They may try to lay the blame on one parent or the other, or else criticise the decisions the parents make concerning home or residential care and their methods of teaching and managing the child. Worst of all, they may reject the child and try to avoid seeing him or involving him in family affairs, visits or outings.

Having a handicapped child tends to limit the family's social life. It may be difficult to find a baby-sitter, especially for an older child who has disturbed behaviour. Sometimes parents avoid taking their handicapped child out with them, because his appearance or his behaviour mark him as abnormal. They may shrink from other people's stares and comments, which they tend to exaggerate because of their sensitivity. It can happen that a family becomes almost completely isolated, dropping contacts with friends, never going out together and never having visitors in the home. In this case it is true to say that a handicapped child has led to a handicapped family.

Handicapped children may mean an extra financial burden. Laundering sheets and nappies, special food or special clothing, replacing any damage done if the child is destructive, can be expensive items. Extra domestic help, plus a baby-sitter long past the age when they are necessary for normal children, may be essential for the survival of the family. The burden becomes worse with increasing age and size. Parents may have to buy clothes and food for adolescents and adults who are unable to earn any money. A few countries give adequate allowances to disabled people but most do not, and parents have to cope as best they can.

Parents whose children are in residential care have reduced but not eliminated their problems. They may wonder if they have made the right decision. They may have the child home for weekends and holidays, with the prospect of a sad parting each time he returns to the residential unit or hospital. These intermittent visits may in some ways be harder for the parents and siblings than if they are used to having the child home the whole time. The distress is particularly acute if the only residential care available is in a large institution where individual attention can never be provided.

SPECIAL PROBLEMS

Autistic children, unless they have some additional handicap affecting their appearance, look normal, and are often very attractive. The diagnosis is not usually made before the age of two or later and parents go through a long period of doubt in which they have a background of nagging anxiety that their child is not normal, but which they try to push out of their minds. They reassure themselves because his physical development gives no cause for alarm and every now and again he does something so skilfully that everyone is sure that he is really intelligent. The time comes eventually when the anxiety is seen to be justified, and expert help is sought. By this time they may have swung so often between hope and despair that they may find the truth hard to accept. The delay in diagnosis also means that the child has developed many secondary behaviour problems which might have been avoided if his handicaps had been understood from birth.

Autism is a comparatively rare condition. Unless they are put in touch with other people in the same situation, parents tend to feel that they are alone in the world, and that no one else has a child like theirs. They feel lost and unable to decide what to do for the best because nothing they have ever learnt about children gives them any idea how to deal with the symptoms of autism. They usually try one approach to the child after another, but give each one up as they do not know how long they ought to persist in order to have any effect. Some parents do find their own way out of this dilemma, but others never find any satisfactory solution unless given the right kind of help.

In the past some professional workers have advised parents against contacting other families with an autistic child. This was because of the theory that the parents themselves were in some way responsible for their child's behaviour. This meant that the usual guilt and shame felt by a parent of any handicapped child was magnified for the parents of autistic children to the detriment of the whole family. Fortunately there has been a considerable swing away from this kind of theory in recent years.

The child's aloofness in the early years causes much distress. Parents tend to feel useless and unwanted. The later development of affection and friendliness when it occurs is a source of pleasure and satisfaction. Disturbed behaviour and episodes of screaming are especially common in autistic as compared with other handicapped children, and parents find it particularly hard because there seems to be no way of comforting or helping the child.

Acceptance of handicap is necessary for proper teaching and management, but this is harder to achieve with an autistic child than, for example, with a mongol child, because autistic children frequently have some non-verbal skills. Parents often feel desperately that if they tried hard enough they could help their child to be completely normal. If this leads to a refusal to face facts the results can be disastrous for both the parents and the child.

Another problem arises from the children's normal appearance. When they show disturbed behaviour in the street strangers tend to feel that the children are thoroughly spoilt. They stare and criticise, instead of showing sympathy as they would with a child who looked severely handicapped. This may sound a trivial problem but many parents know just how infuriating this can be. The naive behaviour of the older child and adolescent is also made to appear that much odder in contrast with his look of complete normality.

To add to all the other special problems, parents have a particularly difficult time when trying to find suitable residential care for the autistic child. Services in all countries are few and far between because interest in early childhood autism has developed so much later than that in children with other handicaps.

REDUCING THE STRESSES AND STRAINS

Unity within the family is a major factor in coping successfully with the strain of raising a handicapped child. In the early years, before the facts have been fully accepted, and when the problems are at their height, it is important to avoid the temptation to blame the other partner for the child's handicaps. It does no good, and a lot of harm, to criticise each other for mishandling the child, or to search for hypothetical evidence that the condition was inherited from one or other side of the family. A series of sleepless nights and terrible days can try the patience of a saint, but the effort of remaining calm and reasonable is well worth while. Keeping one's temper and refusing to nag or become irritable all become easier if worked at consistently. Good family relations have a beneficial effect on the child's behaviour, partly because any child is happier and easier to manage within a united family, and partly because the proper handling of difficult behaviour demands a consistent approach from both parents who must back each other's decisions in front of the child, and reserve questions and discussions on methods for when they are alone together.

A sense of humour is also a great help at these times. Many of the things that autistic children do and say are extremely funny, even if trying at the time they happen, and it does one good to laugh at them in retrospect.

Training and teaching an autistic child is time-consuming. Combining this with bringing up normal children as well sounds like an impossible feat. The only solution seems to be to organise a routine so that the normal children and the handicapped child each have some of the parents' attention each day. A short session with father or mother which comes regularly each day is better than two or three hours together and then nothing more for several days. The parents should not forget themselves in their timetable. They need some rest and relaxation away from the family in order to preserve their sense of proportion. If their horizons are limited to the daily life of the handicapped child, excluding all else, no one benefits, least of all the child himself.

Looking at the parents' problems, an outsider might wonder how they survive and why so many of them positively want to have their child living at home. The attachment between parents and child grows through the daily experience of caring and being cared for. Despite all the difficulties, the very weakness and dependence of a handicapped child often makes this bond especially strong. This attachment has positive results in that the child is loved and cared for by his parents. The negative side – that is, the tendency to give less attention to the other members of the family – has already been mentioned and is to be guarded against.

In the early years, the parents' attachment makes them persevere, even if the child shows little or no response. If he does begin to improve in behaviour, to learn useful skills and, especially, if he begins to demonstrate affection, each small step forward is the more rewarding, because it was so long in coming.

It cannot be emphasised too strongly that autistic children vary very widely in the severity of their handicaps and in the amount of progress they can make, ranging from very little, all the way to the achievement of near-normality. The parents of the more handicapped children have to cope with the sadness of seeing little improvement in their own child, while knowing others with autism who have made great strides. When the diagnosis of autism is first made, all parents hope that their own child will be one of those with the milder form of the handicap, but the follow-up studies have shown that the majority will not be in this category.

This is just one more hard fact among many with which most parents of autistic children have to come to terms. It is pointless for them to waste time in blaming others, or – worse still – themselves, for their child's problems. The constructive approach is to love the child for himself, however little progress he makes. The aim is to find a way of life for each child in which he will be as happy and contented as possible. It is easier to do this if his handicaps and his own individual personality are understood and accepted.

Families of handicapped children need help from professional workers with sufficient knowledge and experience to advise on specific problems and who can work out a general programme of management. The emotional problems in parents that occur as the result of having a handicapped child diminish when they begin to see a plan of action in which they themselves have a positive role. In the next chapter I shall discuss the kinds of services that would help both parents and children.

11

Services for autistic children

DIAGNOSIS AND ASSESSMENT

When suspicion of abnormality first arises, assessment is usually carried out by professionals who deal with a wide range of childhood disorders, of which autism is only one uncommon variety. There is much to be said for centres specialising in problems affecting the development of language and communication. In the United Kingdom, these could be organised within each health region, the numbers and siting depending upon distances and population density. Unfortunately, the need for special services, which are bound to be few in number, conflicts with the need to observe the child in his own home, nursery or school. It is much less informative to see a child in the strange environment of a clinic, especially if he is separated from his family or other people he knows well. The workers in the centres need to find some way of resolving this problem, difficult though it may be in practice.

PRACTICAL ADVICE FOR PARENTS

Parents can learn, from reading published books and articles, some of the general principles of managing and teaching autistic children, but they need specific advice on how to adapt the ideas to their own child. This can be done most effectively if an experienced adviser regularly visits the child's home, and bases his suggestions on the child's behaviour in his everyday environment and the resources available to the family. Parents' groups led by an experienced person are also useful. Co-operation between home and school with regard to management is most important.

Help of this kind is available in some areas, but it is still very difficult for the majority of parents to obtain the practical advice they need.

PRE-SCHOOL UNITS

In recent years, some playgroups, nursery schools and day nurseries have started to accept handicapped, including autistic, children from 2 or 3 years old until school age. This has proved to be of help to the children by introducing them to the company of other children and helping them to learn self-care and social skills. A service of this kind is also much appreciated by the parents, especially the mother, who has some relief from the constant care of the child in his most difficult years.

SCHOOLS

Autistic children need to be able to attend a suitable school from the age of five, or in many cases even earlier than this, up to late adolescence. There has been much argument as to whether the children do best if mixed with normal children, other kinds of handicapped children, or in special schools dealing only with autistic children. It is now very clear from all the evidence that they do best in a structured environment, in which they are given individual attention, later on being taught in small groups of three or four or more as they progress. The teaching methods must be adapted for children with severe language handicaps. The scope of education provided has to be wide enough to help children throughout the whole range of intelligence, from the above average to the severely subnormal. On the whole it is easier to provide these conditions in special schools, but teachers in other kinds of schools are now more willing to accommodate an autistic child. In general the severely retarded children are usually placed within the services for severe mental handicap. The most able autistic children may manage in normal or mixed handicap schools. Those in the middle group, especially if rather difficult in behaviour though with useful skills, are best placed in a specialist school.

RESIDENTIAL ACCOMMODATION

If a child cannot live at home, it may be possible to find him a place in a residential school. This may work well, but some families find the school holidays too great a strain. When full time residential accommodation is necessary, small units run on family lines appear to be the best solution. The child can go to the local special school every day in the same way as if he were living at home. Given enough staff with appropriate experience, some autistic children could live in a family unit of this kind, together with children who have other kinds of handicaps.

Adolescents and adults who were autistic as children also need residential accommodation when they can no longer live with their own families. Hostels for the handicapped within the local community could accept autistic people who have made sufficient progress to fit in. There may also be a case for some hostels which specialise in autistic adults and those with related handicaps.

A few village communities for handicapped people have been developed by voluntary bodies. Some autistic adolescents and adults have been accepted in 'villages' for those with various kinds of mental retardation. A few local societies for autistic children have opened, and others are planning, sheltered communities specifically for autistic adolescents and adults. They are most suitable for those who have enough skills to contribute.

It is becoming clear that such sheltered communities are

not the right places for very severely or profoundly retarded autistic people, especially those with difficult, aggressive behaviour. They need much more personal care and a much simpler programme than the communities mentioned above can provide. The mental handicap hospitals or newer, smaller units for difficult and dependent people should give this type of care. Standards in many, though not all, hospitals are still lamentably low, but parents can work to improve their quality through local Community Health Councils, voluntary societies and by personal contact with staff.

HOSPITAL TREATMENT UNITS

There is as yet no medical treatment for early childhood autism. Most help therefore comes from an educational rather than a medical approach.

Admission to a hospital unit may be required in certain special situations, apart from the obvious one of physical illness. Severe feeding problems have already been mentioned. In some cases, when a child is severely disturbed in behaviour, it may be helpful to admit him to a special hospital unit to investigate the reasons for the problem and to find ways of managing the behaviour. It is most necessary to involve the parents in the investigation and the preparation of a programme of management so that any improvement can be maintained when the child returns home.

VOCATIONAL TRAINING UNITS

Even when an autistic child is one of the small group who can be independent as adults, he will almost always need a further period of preparation before he can find employment. A unit which can provide a gradual transition from school to appropriate vocational training will help to prevent the problems which occur when an immature adolescent has to cope with the adult world. The range of work training should be wide so that each young person can develop his own special skills. The unit should maintain contact with sympathetic employers, and be able to arrange introductions to work in easy stages. The unit should also be closely linked with facilities for sheltered employment.

SHELTERED OCCUPATION

Most autistic adults are too handicapped to work in open employment. Whether they live at home or in residential care, they need occupation suited to their abilities. It would be difficult to set up special units for autistic people alone, but the training centres and special care units run by social service or health authorities for the mentally handicapped accept autistic people. Such a placement is most likely to work well if there are sufficient staff, some of whom understand the autistic handicap.

MEDICAL SERVICES

The problems of finding medical and dental care for a difficult autistic child might be eased if these could be provided at the diagnostic and assessment centres, or at the special hospital units mentioned above. These centres would be familiar with the children's behaviour and could arrange appointments to avoid long waiting times. General hospitals could also arrange special sessions for handicapped children as long as there were staff with a special interest in this work. At least one London teaching hospital has a travelling van which provides dental care at each of the training centres and special units for handicapped children in its local area. This highly successful experiment could with profit be copied elsewhere.

12

The role of parents' societies

Since the last war, consumer groups have started to grow and multiply in Western Europe, particularly England, and in the USA. Among the most successful are the groups representing the parents of handicapped children. The pattern seems to be that the first formed societies represent a wide range of conditions (for example, all mentally handicapped children). Later on, various sectional interests come to the fore, and groups break away to form societies of their own. This seems to happen when the large society begins to achieve some of its aims. Parents of children with unusual problems begin to realise, firstly, that something positive is happening but, secondly, that the move forward is not benefiting their own child. Once this feeling becomes sufficiently general in a minority group, it prefers to leave the original body and start on its own.

Some people feel that this pattern of growth is harmful and should be resisted. The argument against this is that the smaller specialist groups have the knowledge necessary to help their children, and that their needs really are swamped by those of the commoner conditions if they remain within a comprehensive society. On the whole the record of the smaller specialist societies has shown that they are successful in setting up the necessary services. As far as autistic children are concerned, since the first parents' society began in Great Britain in 1962, many other societies have been formed in different countries and considerable progress has been made both in spreading information about the children's problems and in providing schools and other special facilities.

Parents' societies fill a great need by alleviating the isolation felt by families with an autistic child. Regular meetings, correspondence groups, and society news-letters all help to keep parents in touch with each other. Informative talks on various special subjects can be arranged. Equally useful is the chance for parents to exchange ideas on how to solve particular problems, and to experience the pleasure of discussion with someone who has been through it all. Parents' groups are also acquiring experience in how to arrange parties and entertainments for their autistic children, to be shared with their normal brothers and sisters as well.

Informing the general public and people with positions in local and national government, is a valuable function of the parents' groups. Publicity has its dangers since it tends to oversimplify, over-dramatise, and paint too optimistic a picture of what can be done, but it forms a necessary background to community action. Talks, leaflets, posters, booklets and films, plus fund-raising activities such as sales, fêtes and the humble suburban coffee morning, each reach a small audience, but, with persistence, have a cumulative effect. Another aspect of a society's informative function is compiling details of all available services. Parents have difficulty in finding these things out for themselves and social agencies who should help are often woefully ignorant.

The provision of more and better services can be brought about in two ways. Parents can act as a pressure group to put their children's needs before the responsible national and local authorities, in the hope that these authorities will agree to provide the proper facilities. The second method is for parents to raise money and start schools or other units of their own, if this is allowed in the country concerned. In Great Britain a system of 'partnership' between the State and voluntary bodies has grown up. A voluntary society can buy and equip a building to be used, as, for example, a school, and then education authorities can pay fees to the voluntary body on behalf of children whom it wishes to place in the school. This way of working has allowed flexibility and the chance to experiment with methods which perhaps would not be possible in a unit run by a local or national authority.

Most recently formed voluntary societies working on behalf of handicapped children have been started by parents, but are open to interested professional workers. A special quality of drive and determination is found in the groups in which parents have control of the organisation. This is certainly true of societies for autistic children, at least up to the time of writing. Parents on the whole are sharply aware of the needs of their children and, compared with professional workers, are less likely to lose sight of the important concrete issues because of attachment to a theoretical framework. Problems arise when the organisation grows too big to be managed by volunteer workers. Then control may pass into the hands of lay administrators, who lack the motivation of personal experience. This difficulty has been avoided in some groups by the employment, in a professional capacity, of administrators who are also parents of handicapped children. It will be interesting to see how these societies continue to evolve in the future.

13

Outlook for the future

LINES OF RESEARCH

Research in this field follows a number of different lines. Those which are being pursued in the search for fundamental causes were mentioned in the earlier section on theories of causes of autism.

Other workers are concerned with defining the precise handicaps of the children and the way these change with increasing maturity. They are devising ways of testing exactly how the children respond to problems presented to them, how they perceive pictures, or patterns of sound, how they organise their movements, how well they understand what they see and hear, and a host of other interesting questions.

The answers found by those investigating handicaps are of great interest to the workers who are trying to test and systematise techniques of special education. Many excellent teachers are not able to explain how they achieve their success, so it is important that the essential ingredients of their methods should be recorded and used in training other teachers.

Finally, still on a practical level, research to evaluate the way in which services are working is being carried out. It cannot be assumed that, just because a school, an assessment centre, a hospital unit, or a social work service is set up that it will automatically work well. Careful observation by research workers skilled in this kind of investigation is necessary to determine whether a service is achieving the aims for which it was started.

The hope is that the precise way in which autism can be caused will be identified, and that this will lead to the development of methods of cure and prevention. As far as can be seen at the moment, it is likely to be a long time before these hopes are realised. In the meantime, the important task is to help the children who are already handicapped to achieve as happy and as full a life as is possible for them.

PROGRESS MADE BY AUTISTIC CHILDREN

A small number of studies following up autistic children into early adult life have been carried out. The results of them all are very similar. It seems that about five per cent become independent enough as adults to find some form of paid employment. A further 10 per cent do very well, but still need sheltered occupation, at least at the time the studies were completed. Approximately one quarter make appreciable progress but not enough to live and work independently. Some of the rest become less difficult in behaviour, although they still have severe handicaps, but others remain unchanged or even regress.

The amount of progress made is closely related to aspects of childhood development. The more language comprehension and use the child has, the more evidence of some imaginative activity, however limited; and the higher his scores on tests of non-verbal ability, the better the outlook is for his future. The follow-up studies carried out so far have concentrated mainly upon those with early childhood autism. Less is known about children with autistic features, but it seems likely that the same factors will be important for prognosis in this group, too.

AIMS OF EDUCATION

Education cannot alter the severity of any child's handicaps, though it is essential for the realisation of any potential skills. The best analogy is with blind or deaf children. Teaching cannot make them see or hear, but it can, within the limits of their abilities, help them to become more competent.

The content of an educational programme varies depending upon the level of function of the autistic child concerned, but the aims are the same for all. These are, first, to improve social behaviour so that life is easier for the child, his family, or the group of people with whom he is living; second, to teach as many useful self-care, practical and school-work skills as possible; third, to develop the abilities necessary for occupation and for leisure activities; and last, but not least, to help the child understand the world a little better and find some interest and enjoyment in life.

These aims are modest, but their achievement, in however limited degree, is of immense value to the child and his family. Aiming too high, perhaps even assuming that education can make an autistic child normal, may mean intense disappointment and eventual rejection of the child for not having lived up to unrealistic hopes.

The teachers and parents most able to help the children are those who find their reward in learning to know and understand each child as an individual. They accept him however much or little progress he makes. The occasional remarkable successes they regard as a special bonus, but their major interest and satisfaction comes from the task of guiding each child forward at the pace which suits him best.

Book list

L. KANNER, *Childhood Psychosis: Initial Studies and New Insights* (Winston, Washington) 1973. A collection of some of the papers on autistic children written by Leo Kanner, including some excellent clinical descriptions.

J. M. G. ITARD, *The Wild Boy of Aveyron*. Translated by G. and M. Humphrey (Appleton-Century-Crofts, New York) 1962. A description (translated from two works originally published in France in 1801 and 1806) of the education of a boy found wandering wild in the woods, who showed much of the behaviour seen in early childhood autism.

Clara CLAIBORNE PARK, *The Siege* (Colin Smythe Ltd, Gerrards Cross, England) 1968. An account, written by a mother, of the problems of living with an autistic child, and the methods she used to help her daughter.

(There are a number of other books also written by parents. A list may be obtained from the National Society for Autistic Children – address below.)

Lorna WING, *Children Apart* (NAMH, London) 1973. A short booklet describing autistic children and giving some practical advice, especially suitable for the friends and relations of a family with an autistic child.

Sybil ELGAR and Lorna WING, *Teaching Autistic Children* (Guide Lines for Teachers No. 5. The College of Special Education and the National Society for Autistic Children, London) 1969. A brief description of the behaviour of autistic children and the teaching methods used at the Society School for Autistic Children, Ealing, England.

Wendy BROWN, *Practical Guidance For Those Who Work With Autistic Children* (National Society for Autistic Children, London). This booklet contains practical details on what and how to teach autistic children.

Margaret P. EVERARD (Editor), *An Approach to Teaching Autistic Children* (2nd Edition) (Pergamon, Oxford) 1976. A guide to methods of teaching and behaviour management.

Dorothy JEFFREE and R. MCCONKEY, *Let Me Speak* (Souvenir Press, Human Horizons Series, London) 1976. Advice for parents on helping handicapped children to learn to understand and use speech.

Dorothy JEFFREE, R. MCCONKEY and S. HEWSON, *Let Me Play* (Souvenir Press, Human Horizons Series, London) 1977. This describes ways of encouraging handicapped children to develop both manipulative and pretend play.

NATIONAL SOCIETY FOR MENTALLY HANDICAPPED CHILDREN (117 Golden Lane, London, EC1Y 0RT), *Individual Learning Programmes.*

This is a series of five programmes dealing with language, perceptual, sensory and motor problems in handicapped children. They are designed to assist children in overcoming learning difficulties.

Beate HERMELIN and N. O'CONNOR, *Psychological Experiments with Autistic Children* (Pergamon, Oxford) 1970.

M. RUTTER (Editor), *Infantile Autism; Concepts, Characteristics and Treatment* (Churchill & Sons, London) 1971.

Lorna WING (Editor), *Early Childhood Autism* (2nd Edition) (Pergamon Press, Oxford) 1976.

M. RUTTER and E. SCHOPLER (Editors), *Autism: A Reappraisal of Concepts and Treatment* (Plenum Press, London) 1978.

The above four books cover most of the research in psychological, clinical and educational spects of autism published from 1970 to 1978.

A. M. CLARKE and A. D. B. CLARKE, *Early Experience: Myth*

and Evidence (Open Books, London) 1976. A detailed and critical examination of the effects of deprivation in early life, and related topics.

NOTE

The National Society for Autistic Children,
1A, Golders Green Road, London, NW11 8EA.

This Society, the first of its kind to be formed, runs an information service and is in contact with all the other Societies for Autistic Children throughout the world. It publishes articles, and a bibliography of relevant literature. References to the research mentioned in this book can be obtained from the above address.

Index